Autistics' Guide to Dating

of related interest

Asperger Syndrome – A Love Story
Sarah Hendrickx and Keith Newton
Foreword by Tony Attwood
ISBN 978 1 84310 540 4

Aspergers in Love
Maxine Aston
Foreword by Gisela Slater-Walker
ISBN 978 1 84310 115 4

Alone Together
Making an Asperger Marriage Work
Katrin Bentley
Foreword by Tony Attwood
ISBN 978 1 84310 537 4

An Asperger Marriage
Gisela and Christopher Slater-Walker
Foreword by Tony Attwood
ISBN 978 1 84310 017 1

Asperger Syndrome and Long-Term Relationships
Ashley Stanford
Foreword by Liane Holliday Willey
ISBN 978 1 84310 734 7

Asperger's Syndrome and Sexuality
From Adolescence through Adulthood
Isabelle Hénault
Foreword by Tony Attwood
ISBN 978 1 84310 189 5

Sex, Sexuality and the Autism Spectrum
Wendy Lawson
Foreword by Glenys Jones
ISBN 978 1 84310 284 7

The Complete Guide to Asperger's Syndrome
Tony Attwood
ISBN 978 1 84310 495 7

AUTISTICS' GUIDE TO DATING

A Book by Autistics, for Autistics and Those Who Love Them or Who Are In Love with Them

Emilia Murry Ramey and Jody John Ramey

Jessica Kingsley Publishers
London and Philadelphia

First published in 2008
by Jessica Kingsley Publishers
116 Pentonville Road
London N1 9JB, UK
and
400 Market Street, Suite 400
Philadelphia, PA 19106, USA

www.jkp.com

Library of Congress Cataloging in Publication Data
A CIP catalog record for this book is available from the Library of Congress

British Library Cataloguing in Publication Data
A CIP catalog record for this book is available from the British Library

ISBN 978 1 84310 881 8

Printed and bound in the United States by
Thomson-Shore, Inc.
7300 Joy Road, Dester, Michigan, United States, 48130

Contents

1. Setting the Stage

Emilia and Jody present ideas gleaned from their romantic relationship, from the beginning and celebrate what worked best for them and why. It is our hope that this information is accessible for Autistics[1] and those who love them, or who are in love with them.

We are a married Autistic couple. We are in our thirties and we are both university educated. We like taking long walks together and enjoy the arts. We especially enjoy our creative activities together: music, visual arts projects, and performing together as dancers and theater artists. We also enjoy teaching Inclusive Dance[2] and choreography classes to people with and without disabilities. All of these commonalities, and a variety of other issues—some of which you will read about in the next six chapters—contribute to the fact that we are successful in our relationship.

1   The word "Autistic" with a capital "A" is used in the broadest sense to describe anyone diagnosable at any point on the autism spectrum. It is also used as an indicator of an awakening cultural movement in the disability community that views its members as having positive traits. Non-Autistic describes anyone not diagnosable on the autism spectrum.

2   Inclusive Dance is a catch-all phrase that describes any dance class, workshop, or performance that is enacted with the overt purpose of removing barriers to enable people with disabilities to participate fully in the activity.

In our marriage there are several areas in which Emilia is weak and Jody is strong, and there are also several areas in which Jody is weak and Emilia is strong. The traits of autism are present in all human beings (e.g. everyone gets focused on something, or over-loaded every so often) but those who have an Autistic label tend to demonstrate these aspects of their personality more often than those who do not have an Autistic label. To those who are able to make practical use of them, these traits can be a blessing, and to those who cannot they can mean the failure of their relationship.

Despite our success, we make no claim to have mystical under-standings of the concepts defined in this book. We have no innate talents for dating or romance of any sort, nor have we ever found the ultimate resource to gaining understanding of romantic relationships of any type, courting, dating and/or marriage. Some Autistics hav difficulty with processing the non-tangible nature of what is involved in a romantic relationship, and this describes both of us well. We came to a working idea of what these words meant after getting married, following a significant amount of study and reflection as a couple.

Our inquiries began on 14 February 2006, when I (Jody) asked me (Emilia) if we might be willing to submit a joint proposal to do a presentation on dating at the Autscape conference, after only two weeks of dating experience! For those readers who have never heard of Autscape, it is a conference in the United Kingdom that is run by and for Autistics, and which presents practical information on how to use the strengths of autism in life. This is in sharp contrast to many other conferences that focus on how difficult it is to live with an Autistic, or how science is progressing toward a cure, or how to best suppress the self-stimulatory behavior of Autistic people.[3]

Autscape sounded interesting to Emilia. Upon hearing this proposal she laughed, then she accepted the challenge. Assuming we were still together at the time of the conference, we would have several months of dating experience, which would better enable us to

---

3   Self-stimulatory behaviour can include rocking back and forth, flapping the hands, jumping up and down, etc.

offer comments and answer questions. Even though Emilia was willing to speak at Autscape, she was still very nervous. We were inexperienced in dating, in our own relationship and with past encounters. We could not offer any wisdom regarding the subject at hand, only a few survival techniques that had worked for us.

When we arrived at Autscape, it seemed that survival techniques were what people wanted and our presentation was a success. Go team![4] We owe some our success to the conference attendees who participated in our structured discussion group addressing romantic relationships, facilitated the day before our presentation. Doing this reminded us what points we should focus on. Structured discussion groups were held on a variety of topics, led by a facilitator (in this case, Emilia and I), who would ask questions to help keep the conversation going if things started to go "off-track," or if people were not able to initiate communication. It was challenging to lead such a group, but it was a great learning experience. We had loads of fun. The success of the discussion group set up the expectation for success in the presentation. It was not felt to be an isolated success, but the first in a pattern—a pattern of performance. It seems that many principles relating to theater skills were played out here in this example of real-world living.

Finding answers

Theater is communication before an audience, and this communication can occur onstage in a formal theater, or in a one-on-one conversation. The speaker presents, and the audience receives and processes the information. Many Autistics process the non-verbal aspects of communication to a significant degree on a conscious level.[5] For example, instead of recognizing sadness in a person he is talking to, an Autistic may observe the downturned corners of the lips, the eyebrows pulled down, the puffy red eyes, and have to consciously

4   We refer to ourselves as "Team Ramey," because people in general need to work together to have a good marriage.

5   Non-Autistics relate to non-verbal communication well, because they are actually processing it on a sub-conscious level, which is quite efficient.

process what that means. This is inefficient and makes non-verbal communication challenging for Autistics—a skill requiring direct instruction.

Autistic people find the process of learning non-verbal communication especially inefficient when trying to acquire communicative skills in a romantic context. We (Emilia and Jody) have tried to find some answers to this issue in books and articles, but unfortunately there appeared to be no specific articles, books, or sets of books that give reasonable advice on non-verbal instruction for total communicative success. However, it is not impossible to learn some skills, given enough time and effort. We work on this every day, and we continue to improve.

So, what are the possibilities and practicalities of teaching non-verbal communication in a context for romance? We can communicate this best by using a visual metaphor. Imagine teaching a blind person who has never seen red what red is. You can explain the significance society places on the color red, why many countries use red in their flag, and how it is used in figures of speech; but that person will not personally experience or understand the emotional pleasure people derive from that color. However, there is a wide variety of color perceptions, and if that blind person who cannot see red perceives dark vs. light, there is an opportunity to educate that person on how to make extensive use of that information, both in the physical and emotional spheres of communication. Autistics have emotions, but many have difficulty in applying standard language and certain types of social connection to the feelings they process.

The goal of this book is to educate the reader about the rainbow of social perceptions, and how to apply that to the world of dating. We have not, however, produced a social roadmap for interactive success. As a consumer of the information in the pages that follow, it is your responsibility to discern which tidbits you can apply to your own life, making the appropriate changes to your personal lifestyle. There might be three tidbits in the pages that follow, and there might be fifty—it all depends on you.

Knowing that a social roadmap does not exist did not eliminate our desire for such a thing, and hoping to find it, we read several books before we started dating and during the course of our relationship. What seemed to provide the best answers for us, other than trial and error coupled with logic, were stories of relationships written by Autistics for Autistics. These books highlighted the experiences of people just like us who managed to have success in their romantic endeavors. They had all started and maintained relationships despite the fact that many articles by well-meaning researchers claim that Autistics have no interest in romance and/or sexuality.

Of the books that we read, some were written by non-Autistics about Autistics, some covered relationships that were co-authored by Autistics, and other books were authored solely by Autistics and addressed sexuality as the principal subject matter. There were a variety of books we did not like, but on a positive note, we can highlight five books that did have at least a few points of interest for us on the subject of autism and sexuality:

- The first, *Autism-Asperger's and Sexuality: Puberty and Beyond*, by Jerry and Mary Newport (2002) (both of whom are Autistic), is a book that would work well for young adolescents. The Newports focus on several topics such as: bathing, appropriate dressing, and puberty.

- *An Asperger Marriage*, by Chris and Gisela Slater-Walker (2002), is written by a married couple where only one author is Autistic. Their book is an autobiographical work that, in our view, well illustrates possible issues for an Autistic considering a relationship with a non-Autistic.

- *Asperger Syndrome and Long-Term Relationships*, by Ashley Stanford (2002), is written by a non-Autistic who is married to an Autistic man. Her book is a highly detailed work that is good for those adults who are newly diagnosed, or as a good first book for non-Autistics who know nothing of autism and wish to become romantically involved with an Autistic.

- *Sex, Sexuality and the Autism Spectrum*, by Wendy Lawson (2005), written by an Autistic woman, is a book that has a focus on gender presentation, sexual orientation, and self-acceptance, all within the concept of romantic relationships.

- Finally, *The Asperger Love Guide: A Practical Guide for Adults with Asperger's Syndrome to Seeking and Maintaining Successful Relationships*, by Genevieve Edmonds and Dean Worton (2005) is written by an Autistic couple who are not married. Their book gives good bullet point advice for starting and maintaining relationships, but does not give a lot of personal examples.

We believe that for Autistics lots of personal examples are necessary in order to learn how to apply theoretical information. In other words, all the books we list are good (please do read them), covering varied perspectives, but in our opinion, the book you are reading now was a necessary addition to the literature because we include practical steps to take, with significant examples based on our experience.

Some of what we have to say may apply to you and some of what we have to say will completely miss the mark. We have specific sets of sensory hyper- and hypo-sensitivities and our social-skills issues will probably be different from yours. However, some of what we have in our social-skills toolkit might spark an idea for you.

In the chapters that follow, you will see headings labeled with our names. After these headings, we will place our individual stories, which will be told from a single point of view only. We believe it is important to share our individual points of view. We are unique and have different perspectives on the same occurrences during the course of our relationship. We give relevant examples that demonstrate the ideas we are trying to convey in the chapter practically. Since this is an introduction to set the stage to come, in this chapter we include a little biographical data, in order that readers can understand the broader picture of who we were before entering our relationship.

Jody's story

This is not going to be a full autobiography, but I did want to relate some of the challenging aspects of my youth, to show that I do understand difficulty. I am married now, have wonderful friends, graduated from university with a BA and an MS,[6] and have held a variety of jobs. I have a good life, but it took a lot of work to get there, just as it took a lot of work to build my romantic relationship. More details will also come in the following chapters about how that relationship came to be formed.

I have not as yet developed a career, but I think I am getting closer to doing so. I am married and have been since 2 September 2006, which makes me very happy. I have no kids yet and I have yet to start the long process of buying a house. All of this was supposed to be done, according to the life-plan that I composed at age fourteen, before my twenty-seventh birthday! I am now aged thirty-four at the time of writing this paragraph. My life is on a different course than I expected, and it is fine with me now that I have not followed my teenage life-plan. My perceptions have changed much in the twenty years since constructing it, and I know significantly more now than I did then.

Why am I telling you this? I am a storyteller, a performer on a variety of levels, and I come from a long line of artsy folk of one type or another. This is the best characterization I can generate. I am a man who has explored many forms of storytelling—words, pictures, movement, music, etc. —and as an adult I have even combined a few forms, or participants thereof, in the creation process.

Reading the autobiography of Ruth St Denis (1939) influenced me greatly. She talked about how challenging it was for her to separate her artistic, spiritual, and romantic passions. I related to this inability to separate art from other elements of life, and that moved me in the direction of painting in tandem: two people, two paint brushes, one canvas. I also began writing poetry in this manner, and I have combined poetry and painting in a Haiku-like fashion. I am an artist.

6   In the United States, a BA is a Bachelor of Arts; an MS is a Master of Science.

Artists, like myself and others like me, define our generation via the works we produce, and by the labors of those who document our productive output. However, we do not influence our generation alone. Artists have help, and as a young child I was helped through the documentation of my efforts via the hard work of my mother. This is the case with many children. Who else could love a primitive crayon scribble, a muddy paint splotch, or a child-like story about slime monsters?

My mother preserved some of my literary efforts, either by recording or by saving my actual writings. If it weren't for loving parental figures, like my mother, would artists of any type emerge? Parents influence their children in a myriad of ways, encouraging their development as people and as artists, and occasionally bringing up forgotten memories of unusual artistic expressions. Here is an example of a story my mother recorded in January 1978, when I was five years old:

> Someday I am going to be Shadowman and I'm going to have a dog that flies. He will have brown skin and green wings and his name will be Hallelujah.
>
> Hallelujah and I will catch the bad men that live in a house down in Oregon. The bad men caught the good people and turned them into butter. We can turn them back into good people by putting them into a computer.
>
> While the butter is turning back into good people, I will take care of the bad men. Hallelujah and I will fly them to jail. That will make the good people very happy.

I have always had gigantic obstacles to circumvent during my creative processes and the Shadowman story was no exception. When I was five I could read very well, but I had difficulty with writing. This is a negative constraint for one who is born to a creative family stock. I wished that I could write, so that I could create a story. My mother responded, "You do not need to know how to write to make up a story. I'll write it for you." My mother scribed the Shadowman story word for word as I presented it. When my mother acquired a tape recorder she started preserving songs and conversations too.

The reason I picked the Shadowman story to present here is because of the computer reference. In 1978 computers had not worked their way into most businesses, let alone people's homes. My mother did not work in an environment with a computer, so I speculate that my computer awareness came mostly from television. I was primarily entertained by public broadcasting and it seems likely that I was making a reference to a program special on the UNIVAC computer, or an equivocal tribute to man's ingenuity.

In the process of searching for love and acceptance since the age of five, my writing has become a means of self-interaction. I include aspects of my life, and these aspects become more substantial as I manipulate them as literary imagery. However, this stands in direct contrast to my early teen years, a time of producing audio word pictures. This following poem was part of a collection I produced when I was a freshman at Fort Vancouver High School:

> Beautiful the sights
> Sunrise, mountains and prairies
> The orchestra plays

Beau–ti–ful the sights, sun–rise, moun–tains…as you say the words, pronouncing each syllable in a conscious but not exaggerated fashion, feel the sounds; feel how your tongue touches specific parts of your mouth. The metaphor is only secondary. The expression of love is the beginning middle and end, the connection of the story in sound. Melody, countermelody, harmony: all can take me to places much nicer than the daily experiences of life. These places are not mountains, prairies, nor are they lit by a sunrise; it is all a feeling venture, a sense beyond the bodily confines. Even now when I read this, I do not look at the interplay of the standard definitions many people see.

In school I was often the brunt of people's jokes and incurred significant physical abuse. Despite the fact that I enjoyed storytelling, it was music that provided the psychological foundation to deal with the torment I received—whether it was during the times I was talkative, or the times that I was riding on the semi and/or non-verbal sides of living. Going back to Junior High, I can illustrate this with a couple of distinct musical memories which I will detail below: pencil tapping in pre-algebra, and the hellfire experience of being serenaded in physical education.

When I was in seventh grade, in pre-algebra, I expressed myself percussively, because of one of my classmates, Seth. He was a ninth-grader who played in the concert band. Seth wasn't a close friend, but he treated me with kindness, which was better than what I received from most of my classmates (who either ignored me or treated me as lowly scum). When Seth was absent I tried to emulate the rhythm sequences he tapped out on his desk, with a fair amount of volume. It helped me to focus my attention on something positive.

On the negative side of things, in physical education, music was one of several means employed in the act of physical and psychological oppression. I was the primary outlet for many of my classmates' pent-up aggressions. In the locker-room insults flew at me from all sides. People hit me and spat on me. This happened elsewhere, almost every day, but in the locker-room you didn't have the open air for comfort, just the smell of sweaty socks. Music became a cue for groups of students to begin violence en masse. Yes, some of my classmates even went to the trouble of generating a special song:

> Faggot ass, I don't want your faggot ass, I don't need your faggot ass, I don't want your faggot ass, and I'm gonna hit you, da da da da da da. [Yes, they even hit me]

The Faggot Ass song evolved over time and was altered by several of my classmates, till it arrived in this form. At least ten kids, twelve to thirteen years of age, contributed to mold this piece of "art." It was America, in the mid 1980s. The Faggot Ass song was sung in a loud, tense fashion, much like the hit songs of Quiet Riot, Twisted Sister, and the Scorpions, the heavy metal bands that were popular then. I am not sure whether the Faggot Ass song started in seventh or eighth grade, but it is one of my most powerful memories of Junior High; a memory not in picture or physical sensation but in the emotions I felt when hearing the song. Even though I accept myself as a good person now and like myself, I can still hear the tune of this song note for note in my mind, as I write this paragraph. The Faggot Ass song came to symbolize my struggles in the locker-room, naked, unable to run away.

Emilia's story

My story begins with words too, but in a very different way to Jody's. I was an early talker, and extremely articulate with verbal communication. I learned to read when I was five, picking it up quickly in kindergarten. School was very exciting at this time, and I hated to miss a day. We were learning so much, and it was so interesting. Unfortunately, my family moved, and in the first grade I had to start at a new school.

At this new school, kindergarteners didn't really learn anything. I was far ahead of my classmates academically, and the administration of the school considered having me skip a year. This idea was discarded based on my height and/or age. I was too short and/or too young to be in the second grade. This might sound like a silly assertion, but it came up again later. As a second grader, I was very ill much of the year. I still did fine in school (we had barely caught up to what I had learned in kindergarten) but the school wanted me to repeat the year. They thought this time that I was too short to be a third grader.

My classmates tormented me regularly based on my height, and it was hoped that holding me back would end the teasing. I went along with the plan, figuring that it might help. My second year of second grade I was still the shortest student in my class, and my reputation (as someone who could be made to cry) was not unknown to them. Things never did get better at this school. Between the early lack of challenge academically and the teasing, my experience of school was mostly negative.

There was one thing, though, that stands out as very positive. Strangely enough, it happened in my second year of second grade when we spent a couple of weeks studying France. We learned a little about the geography, the cuisine, the culture, and the language. It was fascinating. I wanted to start learning French right away, and I wanted to visit Paris, or maybe even live there someday. I already loved words, so discovering that there are complete other sets of words was like peeking in a candy store filled with untried delights.

French was also special because it was one of my great-grandmother's languages. She had emigrated from Poland, and she spoke five languages, including Polish, Russian, German, and English. We were far apart, so I had not yet met her, but she was still around, and living in Philadelphia. I wanted to speak multiple languages like she did, and be feisty and have adventures like her. She became my role model from a distance, and I loved hearing stories about her life.

My appreciation for good stories came from reading, which became very important to me over the years. Reading was so exciting and interesting that anything connected with reading became special. It provided escape from my anxieties and stressors. (Before switching schools my stressors and annoyances emanated from home primarily: my clothes might have been too hot, too scratchy, too constricting…my mother has a thousand stories of how I was the "child nudist" and how difficult it was to keep clothes on me. If a garment didn't quite fit right or feel right, my quick solution was to remove it. This continued until about age six or seven, when I started wearing full sets of clothing on a regular basis.)

I started to read more and more. I would hide in my room and read for hours. As I got older, the need to escape my reality grew with the increased tensions attached to school and social interaction, and I used reading as an escape to a special reality. Picking up a good story was like going away to a far away place, like actually being in the book, following along with the characters, finding out what was going to happen next.

When I read, nothing would bother me, I would not get hungry or thirsty or tired. I would shut the world out. Sometimes, my parents would call, and I would not hear them. One time, the cat was loudly meowing and scratching at the window screen, and I did not hear her. I was alone and insulated from everything. Reading made me feel safe. I liked the feel of the book. There was something special about opening up the book, the texture of the paper, the "book" smell.

My journey with writing was very different from my journey with reading. Writing was a way to express myself, the way I thought about a variety of topics and issues in the world. I wrote mostly poetry. It was a way to play with language: the sounds, the rhythms, the rhymes. I like that poetry is a neat little bundle of words. It was (and still is) easier for me than writing longer stories. I might lose interest with a longer story, not be able to maintain continuity, or give enough detail. Although I wrote mostly poetry, I really preferred to read books. I wanted to write a book for many years, but I didn't think that I could.

My love of language has continued to the present. When I was a student at Portland State University, I found a new outlet for my fascination with language in working towards a bachelor's degree in applied linguistics. As part of that degree, I also started to study a new language—Hebrew. It was a lot of work, but it was worth it. I find that most things that mean something in life take both time and effort.

Conclusions and joint analysis

In both stories we have illustrations of how sound plays a part in our perception of, and our reactions to, the world. With Jody, the meanings derived from sound are more instinctive and full-bodied, affecting multiple senses, and not easily put into words. On the other hand, Emilia primarily perceives patterns and language from sound. The information she receives through this sensory channel often results in the production of direct and distinct pictures (the underlying ideas behind words), while the information Jody receives through this channel requires more translation and interpretation before he can communicate what he hears through sound to another individual.

These two aural perception types set an interesting, and potentially unstable foundation for the melding of two distinct individuals into a romantic relationship. I (Jody) when listening to "mood" music am not affected by the message on the recording very much, I am primarily affected by the music that is playing. For me (Emilia) the message and the music are equally important in defining the mood. This is one of several potential hazards in our lives together, but keeping this in mind should not dissuade you from seeking out someone with different perceptions from yourself, as a friend or as a romantic partner. (For another example of how Emilia's perceptions differ completely from Jody's, see Appendix B.) Someone with different perceptions has the potential of being a partner with complementary strengths. You can form a more beneficial partnership with someone who has strengths differing from your own, rather than with someone who is a copy of yourself in another gender.

Romance, theater, and social performance

We mentioned the principles of theater earlier in this chapter, and now is the time to explain this more fully. Both of us have some experience in dance and theater, and we wanted to reveal our theatrical backgrounds in a manner not normally seen. Why? We talk a lot about social interactions throughout the book, and it is sometimes helpful to think about social interactions in a manner similar to how you would think of a theatric performance. This is because in everyday life people have to perform certain social rituals in order to be accepted by the individual(s) they are interacting with, no matter what culture they live in. These rituals vary from culture to culture, and they are not static. They change over time.

We give these required demonstrations of social ritual a name—"social performances." Our theoretical model includes an actor who presents an idea that includes all the elements of communication (the person who is speaking), a staged set-up (the environment the speaker is presenting in), the script presented (which are the words that are spoken), and the "vocalics" employed to relate the words under consideration. (By vocalics we mean that the idea is contained in the words, but the interpretation of those words depends on factors such as volume, pitch, rate, etc. These are the factors that can separate factual communication from sarcastic remarks, from genteel humor…)

Every time you present before an audience (the person(s) you are speaking to) the performance is unique. However, despite the uniqueness of every social performance there are recognizable patterns that occur in life and that tend to dominate the interactive stage. However, try not to worry too much about learning the theory behind this model—one needs to apply it in standard conversations in order for it to become easier to understand.

The concern that to participate in the "social-performance model" is actually to engage in lying really could pose a real difficulty for some Autistics, inhibiting their potential understanding of this model. We do not believe that the world is completely full of liars (although there are many). Clearly, you are lying if you present false information—for example, if you say that you are very rich when you do not have a significant amount of money, you are a liar. However, if you are very shy and withdrawn, for example, and you learn skills in order to make a good, outgoing introduction, you are only demonstrating that it is possible for you to do the outgoing introduction, not that you are outgoing all the time.

To carry this further, if you are a person who has "shy tendencies," you can improve your chances of attracting friends and romantic partners by learning how to do a few "outgoing introductions" correctly. Many extroverts are okay with hanging around an introvert if the latter can demonstrate a few outgoing traits, just so they know that, at some level, they are understood. The reverse also has to be true for a good friendship. The outgoing person needs to actively try to understand the introvert at some level, and accommodate their needs.

When later applying what we have to say here, make sure you keep your "acting" believable. What you are doing must portray yourself in a circumstance that is recognizable to you. Do an extroverted greeting that reflects who you are. It is not your goal to pretend to be someone else. If you are a parent or caregiver of someone who is more visibly Autistic, keep this in mind if you take your charge to someone who is teaching non-verbal communication techniques, or verbal techniques. Be sure that they are taking into account the personality of your loved one. Otherwise all you have is script-learning with little real-world application. Practicality is important for many Autistics in having a good day, a good life, and a good relationship—whether that be family, friendly, or romantic.

So, we have now covered the need to learn appropriate presentation skills based on who you are. But we are not going to include a skills list that is applicable in every conceivable context. We have only identified a path, not given you the specific tools that you need to progress on your trek. We will tell you how you can obtain them, but the responsibility for acquiring them falls to you. We are still acquiring some of the tools we need ourselves. Life is a progressive journey.

Things to come

In Chapter 2 we give our definitions of dating and courting with examples from our lives to illustrate how they were shaped by behaviors, our own and that of others. In Chapter 3 we introduce meeting and greeting. Chapter 4 is all about transitioning your relationship from friendly acquaintance to romance, and Chapter 5 addresses how to know when it is best to make such an attempt. In Chapter 6 we introduce physical intimacy (kissing, hugging, etc.) in light of sensory issues. Finally, in Chapter 7 we address the issue of moving toward long-term commitment. Communication is discussed in detail throughout the book, and applications are given for those who need a caregiver to function in most situations. Those of you who are caregivers to Autistics might find a few communication ideas in this book that will be helpful in your own search for that "special person."

When it comes to dating/courting, success is determined more by how one learns to use the communicative tools one can employ, rather than acquiring the "standard" social toolkit, which for some is out of reach. There is a rainbow of personal expression; if one method of communication doesn't work, try something else. There is nothing wrong with that. There will be examples of communication given throughout the book that address multiple environmental influences: social, biological, geographic, and spiritual. This is different from many books on intimate relationships that give general advice for "all situations." Giving advice that is too general does not work and it is illogical to say "always" or "never" in an imperfect world.

2. What are Dating, Courting, and Friendship?

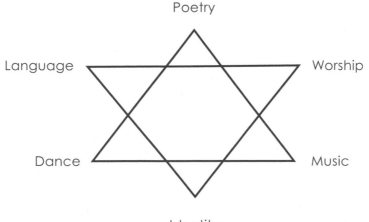

"Image," by Emilia Murry Ramey[1]

Explanation and application

Dating, courting, and friendship are words, and words are sounds given an agreed upon meaning by a specific group of people. That group can be a dyad (group of two), a triad (group of three), the

---

1   Emilia likes to combine art and language in word pictures. This image is a word picture representing the self, defined by relationships: to God (worship), people (language), and self (identity), expressed through the arts. Another example of this is found in Appendix B.

population of a neighborhood, a city, a country…and within the membership group, words are an integral part of the social performance you produce if you are a verbal communicator. Words are a way to express your reality. Words help you and others to shape that reality. You can be different from the larger society, and create your reality, if you find an appropriate outlet. However, finding appropriate outlets becomes difficult for a variety of reasons, including the fact that word usage is not standardized. People confuse words such as: courting, dating, emotional intimacy, friendship, physical intimacy, romance, and so on. Most people are aware that there are differences between these words beyond spelling and sound, but confusion emerges when one asks people for specific definitions of these words.

People engage in physical intimacy and believe they have engaged in a reciprocal act of emotional intimacy—which sometimes is the case, but which sometimes isn't. One person's definition of "friendship" is another's definition of "dating." The words "courting" and "dating" are sometimes used interchangeably, depending on the culture in which they are being used, but often there is a difference in how these terms are viewed. What makes things even more confusing is that everyone reacts to the world in accordance with their unique sensory experiences. This means everyone, with and without disabilities, needs to learn a few common principles for dating and to couple those principles with their unique strengths in order to achieve success.

It is our belief that happiness in a romantic relationship is built on the foundation of friendship. We find that friendship is truly the binding force of our home, not the desire to engage in physical intimacy. Friendship promotes an environment of emotional intimacy, which enhances the peace and comfort of our home as well as the pleasure associated with our physically based encounters. Our friendship keeps us married much more than money, sex, or any ability to make use of hard-to-discern, non-verbal social cues. There are stark similarities between a healthy friendship and a healthy romantic relationship, but there are some important differences that make romantic relationships distinctive and special.

Foundational elements of dating/courting

We believe there are three foundational elements that distinguish dating and courting from other relationship types.

1. Dating/courting has a mental and emotional state that is different from other relationships.

2. The interaction within the context of dating/courting looks different from other relationships, both to the participants and to an outside observer.

3. With dating/courting there is communication and agreement from both parties that they are approaching the relationship as if they are dating/courting.

Many elements can go to make up a romantic relationship, but it is our belief that if you omit any of the three mentioned above, a dating or courting relationship does not exist, even if you think it does. When these three elements are missing on one or both sides, attempting a romantic relationship is likely to produce anger, depression, and/or frustration. Good communication is the key to preventing said difficulties, and this is something that we had both found in our previous relational attempts.

It can be difficult to see from our description of the three elements of dating/courting what is the difference between the two. Many people use the terms interchangeably, but many others also use them independent of each other. So, for increased understanding, we decided to put dating and courting into more of a formal descriptive definition that distinguishes the one from the other.

Dating/Courting differentiated

Dating/Courting is an association (between two humans) with a mutual expectation that feelings of deep affection will be openly displayed by gestures, noticeably different from those used in a business, family, or general social context. There is also an element of engaging in (or working toward) physical intimacy, which can include: being inside someone's personal space, holding hands, linking arms, lap sitting, hugging, kissing, caressing, and/or sexual activity. Physical intimacy in dating/courting is usually coupled with emotional intimacy, the attempt to make your partner feel that he or she is one of the most important aspects of your life.

A dating relationship can lead toward domestic partnership and/or marriage and could be governed by religious, philosophical, or spiritual ways of living. However, with courting there is an expectation near the beginning of the relationship that a couple is working toward the possibility of marriage with each other, often guided by religious, philosophical, or spiritual principles. Courting is often considered to be more platonic than dating, and often involves the active presence of close parental, familial and/or church supervision of the relationship.

As this text proceeds, you will see that our experience leans more toward dating than courting, and so we will lean toward dating as a relationship label for the rest of the book. However, most of what we say should apply to courting contexts, since we did date with the intent of exploring marriage, and we did eventually seek our parents' approval before getting married. If you are a person who desires to be courting rather than dating, please keep reading.

A lack of appropriate information can cause stress, and we (Jody and Emilia), have experienced much of this kind of stress over the span of our lives. Even while we were dating some issues came up that influenced how we perceived and reacted to our potential romantic interest in each other. We did not have shared understanding of whether or not we were dating toward the beginning of our relationship. Both of us spent time asking others what they thought in the hopes of figuring out our status, but neither of us understood what was going on until we discussed the subject together. Of course, having some kind of definition of dating could have made it easier to analyze our own situation and would have saved us time, effort, and anxiety.

A further benefit of a shared understanding of your relationship early on is that if you know what you want, and can clearly articulate that desire, there is a reduced chance of someone taking advantage of you, e.g. seducing you into a situation that you are not ready for. We transitioned into our marriage relationship unharmed, since we genuinely cared for each other and we both wanted to work toward marriage, but there was a certain vulnerability surrounding both of us that could have led to trouble.

Jody's story

It was the tenth day of September, the two thousand and fifth year of the common era of western man. I met Emilia at Rehoboth Messianic Congregation, in Vancouver, WA, USA. I was in a bit of a daze when I met her, because I had just gotten back from a lengthy trip in Europe, where I had participated in two autism conferences, one in the UK and one in Finland, with a month's stay in London between the two events.

I was going through a little re-entry shock, and had a lot on my mind. As soon as I got back, I needed to face the only opportunity that I had ever had for romance—and turn it down. I had met a nice girl the year before, when she was 17 and I was 31, and when she turned 18, she contacted me to see if I was interested in dating her. I was convinced that dating this girl would be absolutely wrong, but part of me, the part that had no success with women, was calling me dirty names. I had wanted to be married since age twelve, but had never even been on a single date.

My long-term frustration was only part of my distraction. I had been in London during a time of upheaval. There was a transport bombing on 7 July, which precipitated the arming of 3000 officers with machine guns to walk the streets, and the profiling of people who were Muslim (or who were perceived to be Muslim, as I was because of my dark hair and long full beard). I apparently got on someone's list, because I was questioned and searched multiple times during that month, and was even taken out of a communion service at St Paul's Cathedral by armed officers. Someone at the London Stock Exchange building saw me walking to church and assumed that I was an Arabic extremist, packing "instruments of terrorism." The police were called. I was wearing slacks and a shirt with a thin tan jacket (not bulky). Isn't racism grand?

This was the psychological background that was present the day I met Emilia. My mind was a battlefield of unquenched desire. Okay, I may have sounded campy[2] when saying that, but there was an intense inner dialog, or rather several dialogs going in my mind the moment I laid eyes on her. Despite this, when Emilia walked through the Oneg room, the place where we ate food after service, I took notice. She was pretty and I wanted to introduce myself. After our formal introductions, which did not occur in the first moment of passing (I was eating at the time), we exchanged a couple of words. I found out that Emilia was new to our congregation and that she was also new to the Messianic movement.[3] I also found out that she was confirmed in the Catholic Church about the same time in life that I was. I was a Catholic who had developed interest in the Messianic movement, and Emilia was just beginning to test the waters, engaging in a similar religious path.

I tried to speak with Emilia on a couple of Saturdays that followed, to see if I could get a relationship going. Since Emilia did not give much in our conversation the first few times, I assumed she was not interested. My thoughts occasionally drifted back to the girl in southern Oregon. This was very bad. Dating the teenager was not the right thing for me to do. Thankfully, all my anxieties were soon to change.

December rolled around and I bumped into Emilia at Portland State University. On that day she talked with me for a couple of hours (Jody's hormones were going wild at that point). The conversation flowed well, which was unusual for me in trying to work toward a declaration of romantic interest. With other women, I would declare interest, and some would not even be aware that I had done so. Worse, some would be annoyed, offended or even frightened. Since things were going so well, I asked Emilia out for coffee and gave her my phone number and email. She didn't contact me, so I was convinced

---

2   Over the top, outlandish, etc.

3   The Messianic movement refers to Messianic Jewish congregations, many of which include people of both Jewish and non-Jewish lineage, who consciously and intentionally celebrate the Jewish roots of their Christian faith practice.

that she was being polite, afraid to say no to me, and that she did not have any romantic interest at all. I was a bit disappointed, but I was used to failure.

Emilia shocked me by asking me out to coffee a couple of weeks later at Rehoboth. With a stunned look on my face I said yes and met her a few days later, Monday, 26 December 2005, at the Starbuck's in the Ione Plaza near Portland State University. We walked over to Portland State after getting coffee and chatted in the Smith Student Union building. The conversation lasted for several hours and I thought Emilia was wonderful! I asked her out again before our first meeting ended. She accepted! We did not go out again till after the new year, but when we did start hanging out, we quickly developed a three-day-per-week schedule. I asked several people if I was dating, and it seemed no one could give me a definite answer.

I have a history of maintaining close female friends, none of which I did anything sexual with, or even kissed. I thought my relationship with Emilia seemed different, but I related to her in the same way as my other female friends, some of whom I have known for ten or more years: meeting for coffee, to do art projects, or to take walks. I asked several people how I could tell if we were dating, and I received several vague answers. The most practical answer I received was to ask Emilia "What is the status of our relationship?"

I had already come to the conclusion that asking Emilia was a necessary component in defining our relationship status as romantic, but questions remained: "When should I ask?," "How should I ask?" At this point in my life I lacked any sort of romantic success, so I had no background to draw upon. Despite my circle of good friends, many of my social relationships were very strenuous for all parties involved. I have even been in contact with the law for simple communicative misunderstandings. In other words, I knew a lot about what I should *not* do in encouraging romance, but not about what I *should* do.

One of my friends, Katee (who was the "best man" at the wedding), suggested I wait six weeks to ask, to avoid scaring Emilia off. This seemed like a good plan, but it was foiled a little early at a hang-out session at Oregon Health Sciences University (OHSU), Monday, 30 January 2006, in which Emilia and I were having a poetry discussion, reciting a couple of poems each that we had written. Emilia was more "on the make" than I was at that time. She and I talked about the possibility of exchanging poems and I said something along the lines of "I have a couple more that are not corny love poems, so I'll dig those up and send them" (via email). She responded approximately "I am okay with corny love poetry." I said something to the effect of, "It might be unusual to send them to someone I wasn't dating" and she responded "We could do that." Just to make sure, I asked if the next time we met we could consider that a date, and she said yes. We did not meet for a week after that, but starting Monday, 6 February 2006, we were "officially" dating. The outward signs of our relationship did not change right after, but there was a change in the way we conversed.

What fascinated me at this point was that I was now able to talk about Emilia, a woman who was becoming special to me, in terms that more comfortably revealed the status of my thoughts and feelings to other people. I was definitely treated better at this point, perhaps as a result of being in a relationship that could lead toward physicality. People did think it odd that a 33-year-old man was not involved, nor had ever been involved, in a romantic relationship. I learned that it was inappropriate to broadcast this information around anyone other than Catholic priests, but I could not figure out a good alternative subject matter in conversations when relationship topics came up. So, my lack of experience came up at times when I did not wish it to.

So, post my dating conversation with Emilia, I began to understand what was at that time a set of elusive concepts: dating, romance, physical and emotional intimacy. Some of this understanding resulted from my romantic experience with Emilia, and some of this understanding was a result of my interactions with evangelical Christian culture in the USA. I had been successful in maintaining friendly relations within this culture but why not romantic ones too? I bemoaned this for a number of years until I met Emilia. Then I had a choice. I understood this framework and was comfortable with the rigid social structure, as long as Emilia was comfortable with me expressing a certain divergence from that way of thinking.

Early in my relationship with Emilia, I was clinging to anything that seemed simple and rigid enough to understand. I asked one of my congregational associates in the Messianic Congregation I attended a few "dad-like" questions, and he suggested that I read about dating vs. courting. I thought, at the time I brought up dating vs. courting with Emilia, that she was a little more conservative than what she is in actuality. Conservative or liberal, it does not matter at this point, because it became clear later on that we have tendencies toward both ways of thinking. We believe that all people have a right to hold and express their views, and that this right should be protected (Liberalism). Keeping this in mind, we do not believe that defending someone's right to speak, exist, or develop as a citizen with equal protection under the law means that we need to personally endorse anything a person has to say or any behavior that is engaged in. We also desire prudence in thinking before any major change is rendered on the societal level (Conservatism).

To give my story a good [time] framework to how we progressed: Emilia and I met Saturday, 10 September 2005; began "hanging out" with each other Monday, 26 December 2005; had our "dating" conversation Monday, 30 January 2006; got engaged Wednesday, 29 March 2006; had our first kiss Tuesday night, 18 April 2006, and were married Saturday, 2 September 2006. Intercourse, of course, happened after we were married. For me, our relationship seemed like a whirlwind, and the intensity was almost overwhelming at times, in a good way.

With successful dating and marital experiences I can now begin to dissect what occurred in my relationship with Emilia, improving my own relationship and hopefully offering insight to others. (I'll be able to do this even better in ten years' time.) I have related my story in this chapter based on the mindset that I was experiencing at that moment, and my perceptions have subsequently changed significantly.

I could go on and on with my personal analysis of myself, but this book is a team effort. So, I will put a halter on my tendency to ramble on, letting Emilia provide greater understanding and clarification of our encounters through the telling of her story.

Emilia's story

I moved to Oregon in October of 2003 in pursuit of better health (because of the milder, more humid climate), and a chance to finish my bachelor's degree. A small part of me also hoped that I would meet a nice man and get married.

My friend Jen from Bozeman was living in Beaverton, and she suggested that I visit Southwest Bible Church. I was living in downtown Portland, and it took about an hour and fifteen minutes to get there from home. There were other churches that were much closer, one just a couple of blocks from my apartment. At first I worked Sundays, and couldn't go to Beaverton for church, but after I got a job with weekends off, I was able to attend regularly. I met quite a few nice people there. One day in a Sunday school class (summer 2005), I asked the teacher if Southwest had any missionaries in Israel. Sheri, a lady in the class who is now a good friend, introduced herself as someone involved with Jews for Jesus. She asked if I would like to visit Rehoboth, a Messianic Jewish congregation in Vancouver, and I was glad for the invite to go. I had seen Rehoboth's website, but I couldn't figure out how I could get there using Vancouver's bus system (Portland's was much more understandable to me). I was studying Hebrew at Portland State University, and I hoped for an opportunity to hear more of the language and learn more of the culture.

Sheri is a dance leader at Rehoboth, so she picked me up in time to get to church for dance class and review. During review I saw Jody for the first time. Well, I saw his feet at first. He has very elegant feet, and he dances well. Later, as I followed Sheri through the Oneg room (Oneg means "delight," and that is where the pot luck is served after service) we saw Jody eating a salad with his fingers. Sheri introduced him and said that he had just gotten back from Europe. He gazed up at us. His eyes were big and pretty, and they didn't blink. I felt a spark of interest and wondered if he were single.

He was very pleasant and spoke to me several times at church. I felt that he must be a longstanding member of the congregation—maybe even in a leadership role. Therefore, I thought that it was his duty to be nice to newcomers. Then I ran into him by chance (or is anything really by chance?) at Portland State University (PSU). We had a nice long chat and he invited me out for coffee to celebrate the last exam of my Finals. This was early in December 2005. He gave me his contact information, but I become stressed when talking on the phone with someone I don't know well. I therefore decided to try an email, but I stared at a blank page for about twenty minutes without knowing what to say. So I tried to find him at his office, but he wasn't there at the time.

I had an interesting chat with someone between my conversation with Jody at PSU and the evening I asked Jody to meet for coffee. My friend mentioned offhandedly that Jody is a high-functioning Autistic. I didn't know what that meant. I had heard the word "Autistic," but I really knew nothing about it. (I was not diagnosed with Asperger's Syndrome (AS)[4] until just before Jody and I got married. As I got to know him, I noticed too many similarities between us to call it a coincidence.) However, at that time I started thinking it over. What do I know about Jody? He does seem different from some other guys I've met—nicer, friendlier, and easier to talk to. And I already knew that he was cute and that I liked him. So I had to ask myself, what's holding me back from getting to know him better? I couldn't think of a single thing, and that is when I decided to become proactive.

When I asked Jody to meet for coffee, I wasn't sure if that would be considered a date or not. I did think that it would be awkward to ask, so I didn't ask. When Jody asked me to meet again, that seemed to signal interest, but I didn't know if he was interested in being friends or in dating. We started spending more time together than I considered normal for "just friends," getting together several days per week. I had never spent that much social time with someone outside of my immediate family before. I enjoyed his company and I knew that just being friends was not my intention. However, I also knew that he has

---

4   Those who are diagnosable with Asperger's Syndrome, have similar manifestations to those with "classic" autism, except they do not experience a significant delay in language development before age three, whereas "classic" Autistics are noticeably delayed in their verbal development from the time they are infants.

a lot of female friends, so I wasn't sure if he felt the same way. I asked my friend Virginia for advice, and she said that I should ask him straight out what his intentions were. That seemed a bit undiplomatic to me, but the opportunity came up in a discussion of poetry for me to express my desire to be dating, and I was bold and daring enough to do so.

Before meeting Jody, I was averaging about two dates per year. Part of the reason was that I was very shy around guys, and part of the reason was that I just didn't go out much, or spend very much time with people. After high school, I alternated between working and continuing education, occasionally attempting both at the same time. Most of my jobs during this time were in customer service, and I was generally too tired to do much outside of work. Despite the fact that I occasionally did go on a date, dating and romantic relationships seemed beyond my reach.

As a college student in Bozeman, MT, I was active in a church that often had discussion in the college group about dating vs. courting, and how couples should go about getting together. Part of the debate was defining terms, to get at the difference between them. Courting was expected to not include any public display of affection (PDA). It was to include much less (if any) time alone as a couple, and much more involvement from family and community. Community service and volunteerism could enter the mix, as well as working together or going on a mission trip together. The male was expected to take the lead in initiating the relationship, since that would set a good pattern for life together. All that said, the root of the issue was the intentions of the people involved. If a couple was courting, then they were serious about the possibility of marriage. On the other hand, if they were dating, it might just be for fun.

I didn't participate in the dating vs. courting debate, but I followed it. My brother felt that they were making too much of terminology—for him it was all about the heart issue. He married in 2005, and his chosen route was more like dating than like courting. When Jody brought up the idea of dating vs. courting, I was not terribly concerned about the distinctions. However, I wanted to accommodate whatever felt more comfortable to him.

My life with Jody has been a series of swift changes. There were changes in my status, routine, self-knowledge and awareness. At times it would have been easier to run away than to deal with it, but I didn't want to run away. In the span of one year (the time I spent dating Jody), I went from knowing nothing about autism, to noticing similarities between myself and Jody, to seeking and receiving a diagnosis of Asperger's Syndrome, to speaking about autism in front of international audiences. I think this would be a rather wild series of events for anyone, with or without a disability. However, knowing the status of my relationship increased my confidence, because I could draw support from my relationship with Jody.

Conclusions and joint analysis

With Jody's story we can see a distinct lack of dating experience before he met Emilia, coupled with a huge focus on romance and marriage. We also see a strong circle of female friends, and the influence that had on his style of communication.

I (Jody) noticed a difference in my relationship with Emilia, which separated our encounters from those of my other female buddies. I acknowledged this when saying: "I thought my relationship with Emilia seemed different, but I related to her in the same way as my other female friends, some of whom I have known for ten or more years: meeting for coffee, to do art projects, or to take walks." At that time I was looking for drastic physical differences, but after the dating discussion at OHSU, I realized that the signs I was picking up on were subtle social cues. One might call them flirtation. I was tuned into them enough to realize they were there, but ignorant enough to not be able to render conscious identification of this relational element, until such time as Emilia boldly encouraged the concept of dating during our encounter on 30 January 2006.

Emilia clarified why she was so willing to ask me out in a conversation we had after we were married. At the beginning of our relationship, I was relating to Emilia in the same way I related to my other friends. However, Emilia had a different perspective. She told me that some of the conversations we had were those that a group of female friends would have, or that a boyfriend and a girlfriend might have. It was this outward sign for her that that prompted her to be forward with me during our encounter at OHSU. Emilia did not realize that my conversational style might have been influenced by my female friends (the bulk of my friendship circle) nor did she realize that I frequently participate in conversations as "one of the girls." Cool advantage for Jody! On the other hand, this could also be one of the elements that caused me difficulty when attempting romantic relationships with women previously.

With Emilia's story we can see patriarchal influences that were a little overemphasized in her Sunday school. Her upbringing was not as rigid as some who have been educated in male-dominated church communities. However, there is a Biblical fallacy that is spread by some individuals and churches who teach that the male must be the leader and the instigator in all things.

Some people look at Ephesians:5, to the segment that speaks to wives submitting to their husbands (verses 22–24) and either emphasize the role of the man as leader and the submission of the woman to a greater extent than they should, or completely stop there, leaving out the equally important part about husbands loving their wives as Christ loved the church. Christ came to this world as a servant-king, leading and loving by moral example. In other words, if you keep this in mind, the husband and the wife should mutually submit to one-another, with the husband bearing an extra-added responsibility for honesty, loyalty, caring…to be the priest of his home.

Beyond specific issues with religious misappropriation, there are also the issues of communication and mindset, and communicating the mindset. Jody had no clue he was dating till he asked Emilia, and Emilia had no clue she was dating till she stepped beyond her religious upbringing, taking it upon herself to examine that viewpoint in light of scripture for herself. Someone had to take a risk, and the benefit of this risk-taking was that it made our lives better. We discussed in depth the difference between courting and dating and decided early on that we were "dorting," a mixture of dating and courting. The word itself sounded cool, but it also symbolized something for us in light of a larger cultural conversation within certain strands of the Christian community on the subject of dating vs. courting.

In the United States some people expend large amounts of energy trying to convince themselves and others that they are not dating, kissing, petting, or having sex, when the opposite is true. For example, numerous sexuality websites have places for people to submit questions, a common one being, "Am I still a virgin if I have…?" We believe if you have written a note to one of these question and answer pages, asking that question, you are probably not a virgin. Many of these websites come up with ultra-specific definitions of what sex is, usually "penis in vagina intercourse" and tell people that they are virgins, even if they have participated in oral, anal, and/or digital sex to the point of orgasm (having anal "sex" = not having sex?). Many church groups have seen some of the crazy dating behavior in America and come up with specific definitions of the word courting that does not include going from partner-to-partner, or engaging in pre-marital gratifications of any kind: kissing, hugging, caressing or sex. Armed with a "new" concept, the churches who are fighting the battle of promiscuity on the linguistic front tell the world to stop dating and engage in courting. Since we associate with and take influence from people in evangelical strands of Christianity, along with our Catholic associations, the question of dating vs. courting was addressed, but not for the same reasons some might think. We were very concerned about each other when it came to conservative views on life, and how that was expressed in the language employed during the course of our conversations.

In the end our environments, social, geographic, and biological, influenced how we viewed and initially reacted to the experience of dating. Coupling this with our lack of experience in dating before meeting each other, and the fact that there is very little written on Autistics and dating, it is understandable that confusion occurred in our lives. When we figured a few things out regarding what makes a date vs. a friend, and established that we were in fact dating, our lives were made better. We did what we could with what we had, and came up with a few definitions (of dating, courting and friendship) in order to provide comforting guidance in our lives.

A note to parents and caregivers

If you are in a care-giving role of someone who is more visibly Autistic, you should teach him[5] the nature of give and take relations to the best of your ability, and to the best ability of the person under your charge. He may never attain the same understanding of romance that you have attained. However, any understanding is more comforting than none at all. Do not conceal knowledge from him because you believe that disabled people can't achieve success in intimate relationships. He will be happier in the long run if he is enabled to live the fullest life possible. Your time and energy can make that happen, even if you need to spend years to achieve this goal. Always progress at a rate that is achievable and never give up! (More details and direction are given on this in later chapters.)

Call to action

Anyone can achieve understanding in relationships, with or without disabilities, and it is a core aspect of our being to do so. Non-Autistics have a social advantage over Autistics in this area, because society caters to their personality type. Non-Autistics receive valuable social-skills training on how to function appropriately in romantic relationships. They are reading books on intimate relationships written by people like themselves. Non-Autistics are receiving instruction (direct instruction as well as indirect modeling of behavior) from parents, family members, and friends on how to best bring out the strengths they have to win friends and romantic partners. Non-Autistics are also benefiting from imagery in the media depicting themselves as valuable, worthy of reproducing, and socially enjoyable.

---

5   We are using the generic "he" and "him" to avoid the awkward "he/she" and "him/her" constructions.

The world will be a better place with the positive strengths of autism contributing to society's social development. To do this, we, as Autistics, need to produce our own books and instruct other Autistics, using personal success as a model for development. We need to create our own positive media coverage (which is starting to happen with both verbal and non-verbal Autistics). We need to publicly define ourselves as valuable to society and worthy of dating. This can be small-scale, or be of a magnitude that receives world-wide attention and support. In other words, the attempt we have made is only the beginning. The next publication should be yours!

3. Meeting and Greeting

"Faces everywhere," by Jody John Ramey

Some people have no idea where they should go to meet people. Others have ideas but still don't know how often they should go or how to prioritize activities that produce better results. Some don't know which topics of conversation are appropriate in which context.

For example, although your favorite subject may be *Dr Who*, or even more specifically, the significance of Tom Baker's actions when he offered jelly babies to someone he met, that subject might not be the best to engage in when starting a conversation at your grandmother's funeral. Equally, there are places where *Dr Who* conversations can be productive as building blocks for potential friendly and romantic relationships. This is a staging issue; you can have the same conversation in two different locations and the success or lack thereof can be completely determined by the location of performance. Yes, social interaction is much like theater. Ultimately, to meet someone and connect, all you need to do is think about what you like to do, then seek out and engage in this activity in an appropriate place with other people.

One of the most significant steps both of us took while trying to improve our social lives over the years was listing, on a piece of paper, what we found interesting. This enabled us to visualize which social activities would be better to seek out when attempting to share common interests with other people. The next step was going out and participating in interactive fun, in an attempt to make new friends.

While you are engaging in activities with other people, you should start conversations with them. Many of these people will not be Autistic. Now, most Autistics don't like small talk[1] and it may seem like most non-Autistics do! However annoying small talk may be to us, it can be useful to get a conversation started. Most non-Autistics have many interesting things to talk about and are more than willing to do so. It's just that they have their own way of going about things, and sometimes need a little accommodation. Connections begin with taking a risk or making an accommodation. This is something we discovered as we progressed in our relationship together. We both took risks at certain points to reach out to the other. Taking risks may seem simple to some, and to others this may seem overwhelming or insur-

---

1   Small talk is the communication that doesn't really communicate anything—just a willingness to interact with another person, and can include such things as "How are you?" "Fine, and you?" sorts of exchanges as well as talking about the weather.

mountable. This was a challenge for us, too, but we have found a few ways to understand connections and express some of our ideas on the subject.

Non-Autistics put out a lot of introductions before they find people to relate with, and Autistics should expect to do the same. Relationships fail for a variety of reasons, some of which are social issues, while others are financial. For example, it is not uncommon to ask someone out for coffee as a means of initial relational exchange. This is part of the expected risk-taking when beginning a relationship, and at times, this might be too expensive a venture for some Autistics, who tend to have a high rate of unemployment.

Sensory issues might be a factor to consider with specific activities (e.g. How loud, how bright, how perfumed will the environment be?). Social and/or anxiety issues might also be a factor (e.g. Will there be small or large groups? How chaotic will the socializing be?), along with verbal communication. Throughout the months that we (Jody and Emilia) dated, and during the first few months of marriage, we had to deal with all of these factors. Despite this, fun dates and activities were and still are a part of our lives, and we still meet new and interesting people to expand our social networks. Being Autistic does not eliminate you from living life, it just provides a framework for living it. There are strengths and weaknesses to the Autistic mind, much like there are strengths and weaknesses associated with any human characteristic, whether it is physical, mental, or emotional.

Weaknesses disclosed

Since the topic of weaknesses has now been referred to, we will now disclose our specific issues in starting, maintaining, and closing conversations. We have them, lots of them, and they have never gone away. Sometimes Jody goes non-verbal when extremely stressed. More often he uses words to create a space around him, and he has developed several compensatory measures which enable him to contribute to a group conversation, even if he is not able to keep up with everything going on in the conversation.

One of the most useful measures is "subject reflection." Jody might miss several portions of the conversation, to the point that he is having difficulty following what is being said, but there might be a point in which he understands that a particular word is significant, based upon what parts of the conversation he has followed, coupled with tonal emphasis on a word, coupled with facial features that might suggest strong emotion.

For example, someone might be telling some sort of story that he is not following well, but they might say that they got fired, with the word "fired" being louder, and their face contorted. At that point Jody might contort his face slightly, and say, "fired" while making use of a tone that is similar to that of the speaker, which can demonstrate that Jody is listening, following along with the story, and sympathizing with the strife and struggle. He makes an emotional connection. For this particular technique, you need to have some of the conversation in your mind, so that you can at least assess that a particular word is important, otherwise, you will be perceived as obnoxious. This is a good technique for those who are talkative but who have difficulty in following messages throughout the conversation.

Now, Emilia is generally not talkative (especially in groups), but she can become overly verbal if stressed over potential conflict, or she might break down and cry. In one-on-one conversations she is able to utilize a technique her mother taught her for continuing conversations: listen carefully as someone talks, and then ask a relevant question. (For example, if someone mentions they just got a new puppy, ask "What is his name?" or "Where did you get him?" or "How old is he?" or "Is he very playful?")

Despite the difficulties we have, when we are talking about things we like, conversation becomes easier. Also, if we persevere on things we like, and the person we are chatting with perseveres on similar topics, we have greater success in communication and social connection. This worked out well for us in our friendships, and we were able to apply it to our dating relationship as well.

Jody's story

Many of the activities that I enjoyed and pursued in my dating life had roots in some of the positive experiences of my youth. For example, I like hard rock and heavy metal music, and have been known to listen to my stereo at high volume. I never thought about going to, or playing in a live rock concert when I was younger, but this changed after I wandered into a hotel bar in Everett, Washington, USA. I was in Everett with my high school jazz band, which was going to play in a competition the next morning. I was 14 years old.

The hotel bar was an empty room, dimly lit, and had a small group of people sitting near the band. I entered the bar and went to the back of the room. A waitress came up to me and asked if I wanted to order a drink. I said no. She told me I could stay and watch the band, and I thanked her. It was a wonderful experience. I was completely relaxed, the band was reasonably good, and because there were so few people smoking in the room, the air was tolerable to breathe. After the band was finished, I spoke with them, and got back to my hotel room at a very late hour. My roommates were asleep, which was good, because they loved to torment me in their waking hours.

This first experience in a bar was wonderful. I was on cloud nine going from the bar to the hotel room. I had a night that was drastically different from all other nights. Seeing the band made rock music human, real. I saw music videos on television, but this was a unique encounter where people treated me with respect and kindness, coupled with a mutual exchange of musical ideals. I did jazz band and symphonic band in high school, and the guy I talked to the longest that evening did too. I had no close friends at that point in life, and I was picked on by every school bully that came along, so a relaxing night out, with positive treatment by one of the performers in this band was intense.

My first bar experience also created a significant shift in my experience of music. Before entering the bar in Everett, I did not imagine myself as a subject of the musical force when listening to rock music, merely an object, washed over by the various chord progressions, noting unique time signatures, interesting harmonic applications, and appreciating a good bass line. However, after my attendance at the bar that night, as I listened to artists: AC/DC, Cinderella, Doobie Brothers, Grand Funk, Iron Maiden, Judas Priest, Kiss, Led Zeppelin, Metallica, Ozzy Osbourne, Quiet Riot, Ratt, Slade, Van Halen, Y & T I would imagine their music coming from my hand. In my mind I would sound similar to the artists playing on the stereo, but I would feel my hands on the guitar neck, my vocal cords tensing and relaxing, etc.

In my high school pep band[2] I would sometimes play the electric bass, rather than the tuba, the instrument I normally played. We would do extended jams that sometimes would drift into the rock arena, and I even jammed with a ska band soon after leaving high school. I was moved to make use of music of all sorts to see if I could generate connections with people. Even while dating Emilia, I would use a variety of styles, including the heaviest of rock styles when performing impromptu songs for her. I am glad I held on to her, despite my wide stylistic variations. (She did not appreciate them all.)

I thought I could replicate the positive reactions of my first bar visit in other bars closer to home, but this was very naive. Bars in general were loud, filled with smoke,[3] and people getting drunk. This was not fun. Also, when I patronized these establishments I started ordering drinks. I do not like the taste of alcohol, but I realized that if you did not order something, you were loitering. I did not wish to cause any trouble.

My attendance at the drinking establishments finally ended, but alcohol was not the factor that convinced me to seek another venue to experience live rock music. It was when I tried to incorporate social

---

2   A pep band is a group of musicians who play at functions or events, like sporting competitions such as football or basketball in the United States, with the purpose of entertaining, or "pepping" up a crowd. The pep band usually plays before the game, the time outs, and at half time.

3   On 8 December 2005, Washington became the fifth state to implement a comprehensive statewide law prohibiting smoking in all indoor public places and workplaces including restaurants, bars, taverns, bowling alleys, skating rinks, and non-tribal casinos. The first bar I entered was almost 18 smoke-filled years previous in fall 1987.

activity into my outings that problems ensued. I wanted to, but it just did not work. Social relationships were extremely stressful for me in bar situations. People would try to talk to me, which meant loud yelling, due to the music. These two stimuli, combined with unusual lighting, and people moving about chaotically, would cause my head to spin and give me extra trouble with my sensory integration issues, above and beyond what I usually dealt with. In the end, I would shut everyone and everything out, and not be successful in generating new friends, social contacts, or romantic interests. Even going to the bar with fellow band students was not a solution—they also wanted social interaction, which I could not give to them while bombarded with sensory violations (loud music, smoke, chaotic movement and so on). Frequently I did not even enjoy the music.

I experimented with live concerts in outdoor arenas for a few years after my bar hopping ceased, and my experiences with going to live concerts in outdoor arenas proved to be more rewarding than attending concerts in bars, or performing concerts in bars. There was less expectation that people would talk, so there was less competing stimulus. The music tended to be louder, but that could be compensated for with earplugs and headset ear protection. When I experimented with attending concerts in the company of others, I also ran into issues of them wanting to talk. I finally realized that for me, rock music is solitary, relaxing, and is something that I do not want to share in the moment. I want to share my experiences later.

I did not pick up any new social contacts in my explorations of live concerts, but having the experience of going to a show gave me more topics to employ in later conversations. Also, my experiences taught me that meeting and greeting is more than just doing what you like and being yourself while engaging in the activity, and in the conversations with those around you. You need to take account of the physical issues involved and make allowances for potential overloads.

To shed further light on the issue of meeting and greeting, Emilia has a different set of issues to share regarding the intimacy hurdles she surmounted when attempting to meet others.

Emilia's story

I go on walks to relax, and have since high school. My family has done some hiking together, but I don't particularly like hiking. I have to watch my feet all the time to avoid tripping, and I miss out on the scenery. I have also been on some group hikes, but for me, that was not a good opportunity for either interaction or viewing scenery.

Wishing to be alone as a child, I would sometimes read a book during recess, and sometimes walk around by myself on the playground. Sometimes this worked and sometimes it didn't. I was not able to leave the school yard, so I could not really get away from my classmates. There were two other girls who would occasionally run up behind me and each grab one of my arms. They were faster runners than I was, and it amused them to run along with me till I fell down. So my early attempts at walking were not too successful.

My solitary walks started when my family moved from Clancy to Bozeman Montana when I was 16 years old. While our house was being built, we lived in town, and it was wonderful to be able to get around on foot. I could go to the library, to school, the mall, the park, or along a series of maintained walking paths. This was a nice taste of freedom for me. Living out of town before, I had been dependent on rides to go anywhere. I did not even feel comfortable walking in our old neighborhood, because people let their dogs run wild. When the house was completed, we were again living out of town, but in that span of time I decided that I would live in town when I was on my own, and get around on foot.

Sarah, a friend from Grace Bible Church (in Bozeman) suggested one day that we get together to go for hot chocolate and a walk around town. That was something that I hadn't considered. It was the first time I had gone on a walk with the intent to connect with another person. It was a method of hers to get to know someone better and get a little exercise at the same time. For my own reasons, I found it to be a wonderful addition to my social-skills toolbox.

There have been times when my life seemed to consist only of working and sleeping. I wanted to have some recreation in my life, but many of the group activities I tried were simply too tiring for me. I already had more social interaction than I could really handle from work. The one activity that was both relaxing and entertaining for me was walking. Living in Bozeman Montana, my favorite place to walk was through Lindley Park and the adjacent cemetery. Next to that is Deaconess Hospital, and I would also walk there and get a cup of coffee. When I moved to downtown Portland Oregon, I would walk around whenever I had free time: to the Rose Gardens, alongside the Willamette River, in my neighborhood, and all around the downtown area. I was fascinated by the cityscape. I wanted to learn where everything was located, and memorize the street names in order.

When I first moved to Portland, a friend from work would sometimes go on walks around the city with me. He grew up in the area, and it was fun for him to be a tour guide for me. It was a chance for him to share his knowledge of the city and see it with someone to whom it was all new. He told me about the different neighborhoods of the city, and about the events and festivals that take place there.

I still generally go on solitary hikes, but now also find walking to be a good way to connect with one other person. When walking, it is easier to maintain a conversation; it is easier to think of something to say if I don't have to think about eye contact. It has also been fun to take my family around to places that I had explored on my own—it is a way to share my life with them.

I also see a social benefit from solitary walks. I am less stressed when I am around people, and because I feel better, I am more willing to try to connect with others. Work is less of a problem, too, when I am less anxious overall. In addition, I find walking a good topic of conversation. I like to describe my favorite paths, parks, and fountains. People will often direct me to new places to explore, and tell me about their favorite places.

When Jody and I started dating, walking and talking about walking was an important part of our relationship. It put me at my ease, and enabled me to get to know him better. Many of our dates included going for a walk, and if I didn't know what to talk about, I could talk about walking.

I have since done some career guidance testing at Portland State University, and realized that most of my previous jobs accentuated my weaknesses, and did not touch on my special interests. Armed with this information, I feel that I can now search out jobs that I would be better suited for. I am hopeful that this will prevent my future jobs from being as stressful and exhausting as my past ones. Now I have a couple of strategies, one to reduce stress and one to prevent it. There is always some stress for me in interacting with others, but the more I can manage my overall stress load, the easier it is for me to push myself to get involved.

Conclusions and joint analysis

Meeting and greeting is about the initial experience with the other, the first impression. When Jody was in the bars he would either push someone away (literally), or react in such a shocked manner that people would think he was either high or crazy. He was so on edge from the stimulus of the establishment that he would send people running away from him (literally). When Emilia tried to join group activities, she had trouble keeping up with the conversation. Always feeling a step behind, she rarely found anything to contribute. People considered her pleasant, but she and they did not really form connections.

People tell you to be yourself when seeking friends and romantic partners, and we agree with this. However, the first aspect of your personality that you reveal to another should be the relaxed, creatively focused traits, rather than the wigged-out traits of autism,[4] otherwise you are setting yourself up for social sabotage. To fix this, figure out what major sensory and/or social triggers are likely to be present in a specific venue, and take proactive means to eliminate the problems before they occur. I (Jody) had to do this in a variety of venues, not just with rock concerts. For example, because of my olfactory sensitivities, I have also had similar difficulty with classical concerts and dance performances (because attendees wear scented products), and

---

4   "Wigged-out" is a slang term meaning emotionally or mentally discomposed. Wigged-out traits of autism could include panic attacks, temper tantrums, biting oneself, etc.

especially in my church attendance, which also included people wearing way too many scented products.

For Autistics, external stimulus is paramount in determining what activities are going to be enjoyed. Enjoyable activities bring about the positive traits that an Autistic possesses, and that is a good time to meet new people. Life occurs in patterns, or at least people believe that it does. In reality someone might give a bad first impression, an Autistic for example, making it difficult to impossible to start a relationship. I (Jody) will still go to rock concerts (occasionally), but not as a means to meet new individuals. It is a place to be alone in a sea of thousands. Performing music is a similar experience for me, whether it is classical, jazz, or rock. I am very choosy about the classical concerts and dance performances that I attend, and church is still an ongoing struggle, but my attitude changed after my conversion experience,[5] so I am now more willing to subject myself to unpleasant environments under specific circumstances.

Not all activities need to be shared. A relaxed conversation with someone in a park, discussing individual and mutual areas of passion, can be just as much of a connecting force as two people who love rock concerts stage-diving together. Two people who love walking can also connect through talking about their favorite places to walk, and some of the places they have traveled to. Some argue that without shared experiences you cannot connect with people. Shared experiences can be wonderful, but you need to pick the particular activity that works for you.

Call to action

We have spoken a lot about meeting and greeting, but the biggest and most important question that needs to be asked is: "Why are you dating?" People spend too little time reflecting on their participation in the world of romance, Autistic and non-Autistic alike. Romance, like other types of relational interactions, is transactional, and

5   My conversion experience involved a complete change of my entire personality, fueled by the acceptance of a new spiritual reality, creating and establishing a new and stable attitude not formerly present.

success is largely based on how you articulate the goals you have to the other in the relationship, to see if fulfillment is a possibility. You need to consistently work on self-awareness, figuring out what you may want, along with what you care about, and what your skills and interests are; otherwise you will not have anything to share about yourself.

Our call to action is a simple one: work on your self-awareness in a conscious fashion. Develop a plan for dating. Revisit it often to update it with new information. You do not necessarily need to have every step of your life planned out to succeed, nor do you need to rigidly follow the plan you lay out. You just need to have some organized information to communicate when people ask you questions about your romantic intentions. This could include a potential date, a friend, or a stranger you meet at an autism conference. When we presented at Autscape 2006, we developed the following worksheet and gave it out to the conference participants, to assist in developing such a plan.

Dating plan

How am I going to increase my success in the world of dating?

(Worksheet Prepared For Autscape 2006 conference by Jody John Ramey and Emilia Murry Squyres)

STEP ONE

Write down what goals you have in a relationship: Physical, emotional, intellectual, spiritual, being *very* specific, and revisit your list often to record changes or new ideas.

STEP TWO

Write what your interests are, physical, emotional, intellectual, and spiritual, being *very* specific, and revisit your list often to record changes or new ideas.

STEP THREE

Explore what activities there are in your geographic area that match your interests and goals. If you know of any write them down now. Find out if they are accessible to you, and attend them if they are.

STEP FOUR

If there are not activities in your area that are accessible, find out what communities exist online with like interests and/or start an activity yourself. Even three people who are doing something could attract more people. Think of at least one activity that you like to do and could start yourself and write that down now. What can you do to get at least two people involved in your activity? (For example, if you like to hike, go around to your neighbors and ask them to hike with you, or hang up a poster in a public facility asking for hiking buddies.)

STEP FIVE

After participating regularly in a public activity, if you have gotten to know someone for a while and enjoy their conversation, and they seem to be enjoying yours, ask them to hang out with you in a non-threatening atmosphere and do something—in public.

STEP SIX

You have hung out for a few times, and the conversation is great. Let the person know you really are having a good time and ask if they would consider dating. If the conversation is great, but you do not want to date them, you might have a good friend. Either is good and should be celebrated.

- Keep in mind: if you are caring for an Autistic who has limited intellectual capacity, some of the information presented in the workshop might not apply. However, you can teach skills that will enable independent sexual decisions and even if things never get to that point, arranging times for people to be with others, especially those of differing genders, can offer some sexual satisfaction, without any engagement in sexual or even sensual behaviors. Women and men smell different, look different, and move in unique ways. Everyone has the right to experience their own sexuality.

We don't claim that our approach, as given in the worksheet above, is the ultimate plan for success for Autistics, or for non-Autistics. This is just one way to map out a plan for relational success, one that we developed while we were dating. There are many plans and methods for visually sketching out your life. Feel free to use this particular plan and tailor it to your specific needs, and expand the categories on the plan as you increase your self-knowledge. What things do you want to do for another person; what do you want others to do for you? (For example, a potential date has to avoid ketchup at all costs or must be able to eat mustard?) This also applies if you are a parent or a caregiver for one who is more visibly Autistic. Tailor-make the plan to fit your situation, or find a model that is completely different. The parents and caregivers might also include categories for themselves on how to teach specific interactive skills.

Whatever you use, we recommend you develop a few ideas, write them down, and update your plan often. The more detailed your plan is, the more information you have to use, and with a written plan you are more likely to follow it through. Multiple studies have shown that if you plan on success, it is more likely happen. Also, consider sharing your plans at an autism conference. While you are taking positive action, you can get feedback, and possibly influence someone else to make a positive choice too. We did not decide to write a book on the spur of the moment. This grew out of presentations we made on the subject of dating, spreading positive messages for others to see. Revisit your successful plans and revel in your pre-conceived victories. If you were only partially successful in a specific plan, celebrate that and use your success as a foundation to readjust your plans for your next accomplishment. Victory is progressive.

4. Friendship to Dating

Mustard is a worthy condiment, but it only reaches its full
potential when mixed with hot sauce.

Emilia Murry Ramey

You have decided what you like to do for recreation, spirituality, and
general personal development; found out what you can attend regularly in your area; and you have met a variety of people that represent
your gender of desire. You have started to develop friendly relationships with a variety of individuals (with the strongest emphasis on
building friendships). Now you wish to transition with someone
from friendly acquaintance to dating. To do this you must develop
your relationship to a deeper level of intimacy.

Part of developing your relationship is engaging in extended conversations with people. We have mentioned before our own difficulties in starting, maintaining, and ending conversations that are
outside of our passionate interests. When it is okay to stim[1] on a
subject we like, we have found that we can avoid this difficulty.
However, you cannot stim on a particular subject all the time and
expect to be romantically successful, even if you spend all your time at
Star Trek conventions talking about Klingons. We have already

---

1   "Stim" is short for self-stimulatory behavior, it is slang in the autism community. In
     our usage, to stim on a subject is to perseverate, to talk in depth on a topic, with
     detailed knowledge.

mentioned some of our successful conversation techniques, such as subject reflection and asking questions. In this chapter we talk about restricted codes of communication, and how using one can make someone feel special. In the final chapter of this book we will also explore sharing the special interest of a romantic partner or friend, a good way to get to know someone better. These and many other communication techniques will help to continually build your social-skills toolbox, something we work on every day.

So, what is the next step? How do you efficiently go from an initial meeting and greeting to having a personal relationship? Nobody has come up with a formula that works for more than a few people. However, that does not stop the hundreds of people who write romance self-help books every year from trying to put forth yet another formula. We will not attempt a formula, but we will give some insight in this chapter as to how we transitioned our relationship from friendly acquaintance to dating, continuing on to the next chapter where we will look at gaining a deeper understanding of transitions on a larger scale.

In Chapter 2 we mentioned some of the highlights of meeting at church, then at Portland State University, than seeing each other three days a week or more. Here we are going to expand upon that story, to reveal a deeper understanding of relationship transitions and the function of our lives together.

Jody's story

It is December 2005 again, I have been trying to talk to this pretty woman at church for several weeks, and she is not interacting with me—beyond her polite nods and affirmations. This is a similar response that I have seen her give to other men in church. Despite the fact that she does not seem interested in me, I still try to get noticed.

Later in the month, while walking through Portland State University, I meet this same woman and we converse for two hours. I give her my contact number and email, and after two weeks of her not initiating communication, I am convinced that she is not interested in me. No more attempts to actively pursue romance with this woman. I am through. A couple of weeks later she asks me out for coffee at church. With a stunned look on my face I accept.

Our first get-together on 26 December 2005 was a definite change for me in thought and deed. I was excited at the possibility of starting a relationship, and I was intent upon asking Emilia out again if there was the slightest chance that she got along with me. My mind was in relationship mode, or at least I was revved up at the possibility of relating with someone over a long period of time. My goal was marriage, one marriage, till death do we part.

Despite the fact that I was thinking marriage, I was not specifically thinking marriage with Emilia right away. No love at first sight for Jody. I did not know Emilia beyond her interests in Christianity, Applied Linguistics as a college major, a potential interest in Library Science as a career, and, of course, the gift of her physical beauty given by our maker. However, I was always on the lookout for a possible romantic connection.

On get-together number one, I was faced with a choice that many disabled people face when encountering a new person. When and how do you disclose your medical labels? I was employed as the coordinator of the Disability Advocacy Cultural Association, which was the students with disabilities union at Portland State University. In my position as a peer advocate of disabled students, my medical labels would have come out very soon, whether or not I told her myself. So it was better if this information came out on my terms, rather than at the discretion of another person. I opted to tell her about my autism diagnosis right away—in a fashion that emphasized my strengths. Everyone has to make this judgment based upon their own situation, because all people are living under different circumstances.

I tried to initially broach the subject via humor. I attempted a sparkling and witty, albeit semi-coherent usage of the English language. My goal was to be impressive, and it seemed at the time that my humor came off as mediocre. However, I found out later that I completely flopped. Thanks to the maker of the universe I did not scare Emilia away. Disclosing a hidden disability using humor can drive away a person that does not know you well. Humor can be taken the wrong way, and can be offensive if misinterpreted, which is often the case when the subject of the humor is a medically related topic.

I found out a few months later that Emilia already knew of my autism diagnosis, but even if she did not, I was in a position to come out of the closet, and it put me at ease to know that in my position as a disability advocate in student leadership, I would not have to hide my identity when Emilia stopped by my office.

My next meeting with Emilia was more than a week later, and a lot happened to me between meetings. On Sunday, 1 January 2006, while walking home from Mass at St Joseph Catholic Parish in Vancouver, I fell down on the sidewalk and broke my right shoulder. My right arm was paralyzed due to nerve trauma, which lasted for six weeks after that.

Because I am a dancer, a walker, a hiker, etc., I tend to use my physicality as one of my tools when I am trying to impress someone; I can do certain activities well. The broken shoulder was a big issue for me. I had to learn new balance points so I could stand up from the floor. I had to re-learn how to get dressed. I had to figure out how I was going to write left-handed and I had a dead thing hanging from my right side, also known as my right arm, just when I had a new possibility to investigate in the romance department. (Grrrrr.)

Nonetheless, my attitude was the same going into get-together number two, despite the arm. I am not one to let illness or an injury interrupt my life. At the time I injured the shoulder, I was told that it was probable that I would regain functioning of my arm, but there was the definite possibility that it was not going to happen. Rather than wait to see what the doctor said in a month or two, I was determined to learn life as a lefty. We had our second meeting at the Lloyd Center Mall in Portland, OR, USA, and in subsequent meetings we made art together using multiple-media.

I needed to be myself around Emilia, maintain my life so I could see that I still had something to contribute to her life. I might have over-exaggerated my personality a bit, or maybe what came out was an actual aspect of my personality, triggered via the stress and strain of injury. Either way, during those six weeks of arm paralysis, Emilia and I got to know each other better, and at the end of January (after four weeks of paralysis), Emilia told me on our outing at the Oregon Health Sciences University that she wanted to be dating me, rather than just hanging-out. For me, this was a definite milestone which I will remember until my dying day, but it did not mark the transition into the deeper relationship that I was seeking. What I received that day was an invitation to transition. Only an invitation.

The deepening of our relationship occurred when we developed a restricted code of communication, a unique communication pattern unrecognizable to outside participants. Through shared experiences and inside jokes we excluded other individuals from the intimacy we shared. People understood the fact that there was an overt engagement in social intimacy, but the fine details of what we were communicating remained unexplained. Physicality (hand holding, hugging, kissing) was and still is an important part of our relationship, along with our intimate desires for closeness, but most important was the intentional use of communication as a means to progressively demonstrate to each other that we were special, number one in each other's lives. Emilia took a risk by inviting me to be her boyfriend, but I also took a risk in actively changing my outward behavior to open up to her on a more intimate level. It has been a progressive journey to make her feel like she is the most important woman in the world.

Emilia's story

On our first get-together, Jody was late, which was a little disconcerting. I worried that there had been a miscommunication on either our meeting time or place. I considered the possibility that his bus was running late (was the bridge up?), or that he was ill. I wondered if he had forgotten. I didn't think that he would deliberately stand someone up—it didn't seem like him.

He arrived about half an hour late, but he had a good excuse—someone had been very depressed and needed to talk with him. I did wonder about his boundaries with other people at this point, and his priority-setting abilities. On the other hand, his willingness to take the time to encourage someone showed his compassion, which is a trait that I value highly. I was willing to ignore his tardiness as long as he didn't make it a habit. Habitual tardiness would have been a warning sign (suggesting irresponsibility and unreliability), and I would have been hesitant to develop a deeper relationship with him in that case.

My impression of Jody was overall favorable from our first encounter. I was able to talk to him on a variety of subjects: the arts, higher education, good places to walk in the Portland area. I could talk at length on a subject and not fear that I was boring him. This meant a lot to me, since I generally had trouble talking to guys.

When Jody and I started hanging-out, I already knew that he had a diagnosis on the autism spectrum. So his disclosure was not news to me. It was just as well, because he was rather blunt in telling me, and at the time, I was concerned that I might have offended him. He had started by telling me that he is gluten-intolerant, and when I suggested that must be difficult for him, he asked rather abruptly, "Why, because I am a high-functioning Autistic?" I thought that he might be overly sensitive about his disability, but I certainly did not wish to offend him.

Overall, he seemed very sweet, and easy to get along with, and I wanted to get to know him better. I don't know how much my knowledge of his disability affected my reactions to him. I thought it was a little unfair that he had not had the chance to disclose his own diagnosis because I had learned of it elsewhere first. At the time I wondered if that might have made me overlook certain things, like his tardiness to our first meeting. After considering the matter, though, I don't think that is the case. I had already observed some traits in him that I really value. His intelligence, kindness, and sense of humor were endearing.

When Jody broke his shoulder, I was concerned for him, and found myself praying for him frequently, for his speedy healing, for rest at night, and for peace of mind. During the day, I often thought to pray for his recovery, and whenever I woke at night, I would ask for a pleasant night's sleep for him. During this time, my respect and admiration for him increased dramatically. What I appreciated was his ability to make the injury into a learning experience, even an adventure. He did not complain, question God, or become lazy. His attitude was extremely attractive. Because of the way he handled his injury, I was confirmed in my good opinion of Jody. Because of the time spent praying for him, I also felt more strongly toward him.

When Jody and I met, I had no idea that I myself would be diagnosed with Asperger's. Part of getting to know him was also getting to know myself. The day we met at OHSU (30 January 2006), we talked over many similar aspects in our lives. Looking back for a moment, it was as if order had been imposed over the apparent randomness of my life. Jody did not suggest that I could be an "Aspie," and I told myself that as long as he didn't notice, it was all an invention of my imagination. However, I knew that to deepen my relationship with Jody meant to face the part of myself that might be disabled. It was both exciting and scary, but I had reached a point where I really wanted my life to be meaningful rather than easy. I looked back on a pattern of failure, of quitting, and of going from one meaningless job to the next. I knew that I didn't want that for my life. That's why I went back to school, and that's why I didn't run away from a romantic relationship with Jody. Dating Jody meant that I was ready to face the fear of my own personality.

On Valentine's Day, we went shopping at the Lloyd Center Mall. This day we wandered around to different stores and went up and down the escalators. A couple of times we stood close together and I didn't have the fight or flight response that I frequently had in the past with other men, and I wasn't even annoyed. I wasn't tempted to slap or punch him. In fact, it was very nice to be close together and this was also a positive sign for me. I knew then that I was physically attracted to Jody, which was an important factor in my opening up to him and increasing my vulnerability.

This physical/emotional connection was influenced by a marriage and family class I took at Montana Bible College. The teachers (this class was taught by a married couple) told the story of a couple who got married without being attracted to each other physically. It ended badly, with the wife leaving her husband and their children for a man that she was attracted to. Our teachers emphasized that physical attraction is an important element in a romantic relationship. The physical side of love is good and healthy, designed by God, and ignoring that factor in looking for a mate is not wise.

Conclusions and joint analysis

One of the main points to our stories here is the fact that our relationship status had not changed significantly when we said we were going to be dating. We wanted it to, but the change came for us when we altered our behavior to engage in a deeper level of emotional intimacy, making the attempt to prioritize each other as the number one person in each other's lives.

For Emilia it occurred soon after our Valentine's Day encounter when Jody was standing close to her and she didn't have a fight or flight reaction. This told her that she was physically attracted to him in a way wholly separate from just thinking he was cute. She opened up to him more after that encounter, which was a significant relational hook. Now, when we say that for Emilia there were more physical manifestations guiding her choice than there were for Jody, that does not mean she was making a choice solely on the basis of a hormonal reaction. The reality of the situation is, for Jody and for a lot of other men, thinking that a woman is cute is also an indicator of physical attraction. For Emilia, and a number of other women, there must be a greater emotional connection to indicate physical attraction, which means that thinking someone is cute and being attracted to them physically are two separate things.

Jody already came to the conclusion that he was physically attracted to Emilia long before the first get-together, so he was only looking for the emotive connection, while Emilia was looking for both. For Jody, the transition from friendly acquaintance to romance and a deeper connection had little to do with physicality. It had more to do with conversational connection, as Emilia and he developed a restricted code of communication.

What is a restricted code of communication? It is a sub-dialect that is only understood by a small group of individuals. In the case of romantic relationships, a restricted code would just be understood by you and your significant other. When spending a lot of time with someone, and having a lot of shared experiences, you have a significant body of reference points to address when you communicate with each other. This communication, if intentionally used, can be a way to signify to the other that they are special. You are only communicating with them and no one else. The phrases you say might even sound funny to an outsider, but will hold significant meaning to those using their personal sub-dialect.

The key to using a restricted code of communication is to use these unique phrases you generate as a means to remind your loved one of a funny experience, a romantic experience, anything that would be a memory enhancer that only you two can understand. For example, we (Jody and Emilia) have given names to places of significance, which bear no common attachment to the actual name of those locations: "Grand Central Station," "The Clubhouse," and "Bog of Eternal Stench." The memories are the guiding principle, not the grammatical structure, or even the idiomatic expression.

The restricted code between partners can and will change and expand over time. This is okay. There is a power in language that enables you to go to a peaceful place with someone else, a joint form of stimulation.

Back to the analysis of our stories.

Another of the main points that both stories illustrated was that disability had an impact on our relationship, from the very beginning and that had both positive and negative manifestations. For example, I (Jody) was too blunt in my disclosure of my disability. The negative views surrounding disability itself and my presentation of it could have been the end of any possible relationship, before it started.

On the flip side, because of the negativity surrounding disability, and the fact that someone told Emilia that Jody was Autistic before the first get-together, it gave Emilia lower expectations upfront, which helped with the unexpected tardiness on 26 December. As Emilia confronted the possibility that she was an Aspie over the next few months, having conversation after conversation with Jody about all aspects of disability, her views gradually changed from a negative view of disability, to one where the defined traits of a specific diagnosis are a gift from our maker.

When we speak of disability, we are speaking of a social model of disability that presents itself with medically defined characteristics. We opt for this rather than looking at some of the legally accepted definitions that concentrate on the biological organism only. Forgetting that individuals live in a structured society, and that these individuals are human beings with unique manifestations of their impairments, is in our belief indecent and offensive.

A disability is a set of behavioral and/or biological traits that are medically defined and societally devalued. We use the word "disability" because through either direct or indirect actions, on a systematic level, a society dis-ables a specific set of people from engaging in certain types of activities. In one society, people with certain traits are highly valued, and in another, people with those same traits are institutionalized. Autism is not a universal diagnostic category around the world. Even in countries where the medical establishment recognizes autism, its definition has changed through multiple editions of the DSM,[2] the ICD,[3] and other major reference works.

Jody, through contact with Autistic self-advocates, had overcome most of his negative views of disability. Still, he probably overcompensated when he broke his shoulder, going so far as to work as a performer and a choreographer on a dance film, *Transitions*, which was funded by the Regional Arts and Culture Council. He performed about twelve minutes of choreography with two other dancers all with an un-casted broken shoulder. Emilia changed many of her views through our dating relationship, but strangely enough, society's negativity may have contributed to our getting together.

2   *Diagnostic and Statistical Manual of Mental Disorders* (American Psychiatric Association). Definitions and descriptions of autism and related labels have been changed multiple times over various editions since DSM III was released in 1980, recording the first entry of autism in this text.

3   *International Classification of Diseases* (World Health Organization). Definitions and descriptions of autism and related labels have been changed multiple times since ICD 8 was released in 1965, recording the first entry of autism in this text.

Call to action

We have mentioned in various points the value of friendship in romantic relationships, but have not yet developed that topic here in print. This is a dating book, not a book on friendship. However, friendship is the foundation of a good romantic relationship and/or marriage. Also, if you have multiple friends, you can talk about some of the intense feelings generated by your romantic relationships. Friends can give you perspectives on how to deal with your feelings more effectively, and reassure you that you are not alone in your dating experiences, whether or not those friends are Autistic. It is helpful to develop friendships with people who have some romantic experience. If you are a parent or caregiver of someone who is more visibly Autistic, you can help to arrange activities with people who are successful in their romantic relationships, so that the person under your charge has more role models to follow. Such friends can provide very valuable support, but even if they have no experience with romance, good friends are helpful to consult for an outside opinion.

All this being said, if you do not have a set of good friends then finding one is more important than seeking out someone to date. You should concentrate your efforts on this before you actively begin searching out a romantic partner. A friend is someone more than a person you work with. A friend is a person who likes to talk to you and spend time with you. Another good indicator of friendship is if they are also helpful, for example, offering to help you move your stuff into a new flat if you change living quarters. You need people like this in your life, and seeking them out involves activities similar to seeking out romantic dates: deciding what you like to do, where you can do this frequently, going out to do this, and engaging people in conversations that are participating in the activity with you. If a certain person or group of individuals seems to fancy having you around, hang out with them in another location, at another time, with the intent of developing a friendship, not a romantic partnership.

Some of the activities that might surround the development of dating also overlap friendship development, so, for the sake of brevity, we will give the activity suggestion list for dating we gave at our Autscape presentation in 2006.

Starting the relationship

- In the first few conversations, have a reason to chat.

- Chat about what you both like. (Try meeting through shared interests.)

- When meeting alone, go to places where you can chat and/or engage in shared interests.

- Don't participate in activities that cause issues with sensory hypersensitivities and/or sensory-integration issues.[4]

- Talk about physical intimacy before you engage in such behaviors.

- Ask before initiating physical intimacy.

- "No" means "no."

- Do something different (e.g. if you are both university students and see each other a lot at the university, go somewhere else every so often).

- If you are both spiritual practitioners, pray/meditate together.

- If you are both spiritual practitioners, go to church/synagogue/mosque/etc. together.

- Remember funny statements, funny moments, and/or significant events in your relationship and bring them up in conversation periodically.

---

4   A sensory-integration issue occurs when the brain is unable to accurately process the information coming in from the senses. Individuals may be *oversensitive* to some sensations, *undersensitive* to some sensations, a combination of both, or can have issues with the *vestibular* sense, which tells us where our body is in space, or the *proprioseptive* sense, which tells us what position our body is in.

- Check in with one another frequently about the relationship and *do not* feel like you have to be like everyone else.

- Always be prepared for the responsibilities of sexuality.[5]

Most of these apply to both friendship and romance, barring the sexual aspects. If a friend is trying to become sexual, they are attempting to transition the relationship into something else. If the sex is forced, it is rape. If the person is seeking consent, you can either agree to a transition or let them know that you only want to be friends.

We do make adjustments from conference to conference in our presentation material, since we are always picking up new tidbits, but the message is largely the same in principle, and is well received wherever we go. For example, after our dating presentation at the Biennial Australian Conference on Autism Spectrum Disorders (March 2007), several parents quickly made their way to talk to Emilia while the next speaker was setting up.[6] The parents were very happy to hear a positive message on relationships, feeling discouraged in part by the media and in part by the traits of autism manifested in their children. Parents need to be reminded that Autistic children have the ability to gain social skills and relational success over time—just like many non-Autistic children do. Who can look at an eight-year-old child and say, that person, without change, maturation, and growth, would be successful in marriage? No one!

Summation

Our call to action in this chapter might seem to weigh down the quest for romance with a lot of unnecessary activity, but when you see the benefits of having good friends in your life, you will be much more likely to have a romantic partner involved with you. Potential dates

---

5   The responsibilities of sexuality include taking precautions to avoid sexually transmitted diseases and pregnancy, and to deal with the consequences if they are not avoided.

6   They couldn't come up to Jody because he was presenting from the USA via internet videoconferencing. We were together via technology, but not in physicality.

will see that you are an engaged, socially involved individual. By demonstrating your resources, you will increase your romantic success, as people will be less apt to concentrate on your shortcomings. If you are a caregiver of someone more visibly Autistic, you can arrange successful gatherings of individuals, whether it be one-on-one, online, playing video games—whatever is most likely to help the individual you are involved with become more socially engaged. Start teaching concepts about friendship and romance early in life, and never stop the education process. Possessing knowledge increases the ability to make good judgments. When relating to other people, platonically or not, good judgment can be a cornerstone for safe and healthy living.

5. When Should You Adjust Your Relationship Status?

"The road goes ever on" by Emilia Murry Ramey

A relationship has been started. So how does one know when to transition from friend to romance, or whether, indeed, you should? How can Autistic people answer these questions when non-Autistics have never come up with a decent answer other than "you just know." We (Emilia and Jody) believe that Autistics can shed light upon the subject of transitions in relationships, using our superior Autistic logic. [Emilia and Jody laughing] We are not saying that we have the ultimate answers, because we absolutely do not. However, we are proposing some tangible advice in this chapter that can be built upon in future books. That way, the next Autistic couple who writes a dating book will have less ground to cover.

In the call to action in Chapter 3, we talked about setting up a pre-dating plan that one can continue to revisit. This plan should talk about things you like and dislike. This is only the beginning. Eventually, you want to build your plan to the point that you know what you want from another person, which may include: sharing activities with you, talking to you in a specific way, attending a specific church, having a specific type of employment, or specific level of maturity. If you know what elements are important to you, and you see them present in a particular individual, that is a good sign. You may then want to transition to a deeper level of relating to that person.

Even more important is knowing what you want to give, what you are willing and able to give, and what you do not want to give in a relationship. Because many Autistics deal with sensory reaction so much on a conscious level, it might not be as hard for us to identify what we *want* out of a relationship, but giving is just as important as receiving. If you do not identify what you are able to give, it is possible to get in a position where you are expected to provide something you cannot provide. In that case your relationship could be in serious jeopardy.

Other influencing factors could include family, friends, and religious leaders. Your family has the potential of knowing you better than you know yourself—if you have lived with them a good portion of your life. If a large percentage of your family and friends are saying that a person is right for you, that is good. It can be another possible indicator to proceed with that individual to another level in your relationship. Religious leaders have the authority to make religious interpretations based on the traditions they serve in, and could also advise you on a potential romantic partner. All of this together sets the scene for connecting your relationship to the community in which you live. This will be addressed to a certain extent in this chapter, but will receive in-depth treatment in the final chapter of this book.

A lot of what we say in our stories in this chapter involve the "how" of relationship transition, but the "how" part must be there to provide the foundation to explore the "when and why." Many people talk about timing in relationships, and timing, even if all other aspects are there, can make or break any type of relationship, for people with or without disabilities. Pay very close attention to some of the intricacies of this chapter, and you might see some very immediate changes in the success of your relationship transitions.

Jody's story

I have wanted to be married since I was 12 years old. I cannot describe the pull logically, nor can I describe my relationship with Emilia in a purely logical fashion. A certain amount of romance is irrational, especially when you get to the point when you are "falling in love" with a person. Studies have shown that there are so many chemicals being shot off in your body during this process that, for a few months, it is like you are high on drugs, only without the bad side-effects. Having being in that position, I agree.

There were little experiences, like hand-holding, that at times became explosively pleasurable. The intensity of these experiences did not promote clear thinking. This, paired with my logical foundation, provided the basis for my decision to progress in my relationship with Emilia. My first impression of Emilia was that she was a beautiful woman with a shapely body, and I was physically excited that she was talking to me. This was before our first get-together at PSU, when we were only exchanging a few words at church.

What I am speaking of here are my desires: my desire to marry since age twelve, my desires relating to Emilia's physical form before and after dating her, and my desires for even more pleasure when Emilia and I held hands (after beginning our dating relationship). Desires are natural, normal, and can be exciting to experience. However, desires do not indicate readiness to participate in a relationship of any sort, nor do they indicate appropriate timing to progress from friend to dating, from dating to engagement, or engagement to marriage. Furthermore, desires do not indicate readiness to indulge in, nor incite further desire.

When Emilia and I started meeting by ourselves on 26 December 2005 I was determined to encourage romance with her. This stubborn attitude was not wise, as it could have led to a failed relationship. Things worked out for us, but I should have concentrated on what I wanted out of a relationship, and what I was able to give, right from the beginning. That way, in case our relationship was not going to work, it could have ended efficiently, reducing potential heartbreak. Eventually I shifted into my logical mode of thinking, but it wasn't till February before we saw any of that float to the surface.

Many good things happened for me at the start of the Ramey relationship. Because I have wanted to be married since the age of 12, and had no dating experience between 12 and 32, I had a lot of time to think about what would be the benefits and drawbacks of getting married, and what I wanted out of a relationship. I also had time to develop several significant friendships along the way, giving me a good foundation of emotional support before delving in to a relationship of higher significance. This made my first dating relationship (with Emilia, who is now my wife) much better than it probably would have been if I had not had such a good foundation in my circle of friends.

I wanted Emilia to be my friend, as well as my girlfriend, so I went into my dating relationship with a decision that I was not going to engage in sexual activity, and I am thankful that I made that decision. I found out during the course of our dating relationship that minor expressions of physical intimacy were very intense, so I was glad I had made the choice to save certain things for marriage. I am not saying this just because of my Christian beliefs, but also because indulging in significant amounts of intense pleasure too early can inhibit sound judgment.

Emilia was upfront about physical expression, and wanting to go slowly. This was something very tangible that suggested to me that Emilia would be a good match as a romantic partner. She knew what she wanted, and it meshed with what I wanted. As we progressed and started getting to know each other in a variety of social situations, I found that we had a lot of common interests—faith, the arts, the value of people—and through our get-togethers, and through our romantic dating period, I discovered that Emilia and I worked well with each other as a team in a variety of situations.

Emilia volunteered with the Disability Advocacy Cultural Association, when I was the coordinator, and got involved with our Inclusive Dance team. We coached each other a little bit on our homework assignments, and we also worked together on our first dating presentation that we gave at the Autscape conference, August of 2006.

As we previously mentioned, I asked Emilia if she would be interested in doing a presentation on dating at the Autscape conference in the United Kingdom. I did this on our Valentine's date at the Pioneer Place Mall in Portland. We had only been officially dating for a couple of weeks, and Emilia was a little hesitant, because she thought there was nothing she could offer on the subject of dating, due to her lack of experience with dating, her lack of knowledge of autism, and the fact that, as she told me at the time, "I am not an Autistic." I told her that by dating one she would know more than what the self-proclaimed experts[1] know. After a little cajoling she laughed and accepted the challenge.

This was a big indicator to me that Emilia would be a good match for me. She was willing to do something that society would deem a little out of the ordinary. Here we were, two college students with no money, talking about traveling to an international conference together to talk about something we had little to no awareness of or experience with. Emilia showed me that she was willing to think outside the box, and make personal investments toward our future. Working together over the next few months on the logistical issues of international travel and putting together a 1.5 hour presentation tested Emilia's desire and revealed her tendencies to be a team player. She passed with flying colors.

---

1   It is my opinion that there are no experts in the autism universe. We all can and should learn from each other: whether someone has a PhD in psychology, is a parent of an Autistic, or if someone is Autistic themselves.

Putting all this together, and relating the events that led to me knowing the appropriate time for me to transition from friendly acquaintance to romance was then, and still is, hard. When Emilia and I first started hanging-out, I was attempting to develop our relationship as far as possible, because there was evidence that she seemed interested, and I was "on the make." After I received the invite to be her boyfriend, I started paying close attention as to whether or not she matched up with my needs, wants, and desires. A pretty face can only hold your interest for so long. You need some common dreams and goals if a relationship is actually going to work in the long term.

For me, the first milestone of transition into a deeper relationship would have to be our dating discussion at OHSU, because that was the wake-up call. The second milestone would be on Valentine's Day, when we were eating lunch in the food court at the Pioneer Place Mall discussing Autscape, because that was her demonstration of thinking outside the box. This occurred after several wonderful conversations in person and on the phone where we cohesively matched up on a myriad of topics.

The third milestone occurred at my friend Stacy's house. My friends Katee, Stacy, and Stacy's parents, Rick and Lorene, along with Emilia and I, watched a Heffalump movie together and I made the big introduction of my new girlfriend Emilia. We chatted for a while after the movie was over and had a good time. It was the beginning of connecting the idea of intimate relationships to my circle of friends. Katee and Stacy, two of my "groomsmen" at the wedding, approved of Emilia, and decided she was good company to keep.

The final milestone was on Monday, 27 February 2006, in the afternoon, when Emilia and I decided to leave the Portland State University campus and go for a walk in the Royal Rosarian Gardens in Washington Park. This was the first day that we held hands. Until this day we had not touched each other beyond an accidental bump, or, in my case, a couple of purposeful blunders to gain some contact. (Don't tell Emilia!) She brought up some research she had read about Autistics not liking to have physical contact and that blended into a conversation about holding hands. For me this was the last major milestone and I started opening up a lot more after this.

Emilia's story

When I was in high school, I decided that I wanted to be a nun. I had it all figured out logically: A career woman works for a company and is rewarded with money, a wife works for a husband and is rewarded with love, and a nun works for God and is rewarded with peace. Then I considered the possibilities of these three paths. Some career women are mistreated, underpaid, or even fired. Some wives are not loved. On the other hand, God is eternally faithful. It made perfect sense—at the time.

I did not end up becoming a nun because I did not actually have a call from God to do so. I did not think that marriage was really open to me, having been told many times that no man would ever want me. That left one path, the career. I went from one job to another, trying to find something that could become long term. I couldn't see any future in any of the jobs I tried. This led me to return to school, and to be much more serious about studying than I had been in high school. I hoped that once I finished my bachelor's degree in Applied Linguistics, there would be some job available that I would really like, and I could settle down and be a good career woman.

Before I finished school, I met a nice guy at church. At this time, I started to see more options for life. I hadn't previously participated in Inclusive Dance (dance for people with and without disabilities), or thought about speaking at conferences, or done any advocacy work. I knew very little about the disability community, and almost nothing about autism.

There were many transitions in my life during this time, and most of them were linked to my relationship with Jody. The first relationship transition for me was the conversation at PSU. Previous to that day, I had considered Jody's friendly behavior to be nothing more than a long-time member of a church trying to make a new person feel welcome. When he took the time to talk to me in a different setting, I realized that he might actually like me. The second transition was our discussion at OHSU, when we were comparing events in our childhood, and talking about similarities in our lives. When I saw the similarities, my first thought was that Jody couldn't really be on the autism spectrum, because he had so much in common with me. I said to myself, "I am certainly not autistic." because "If I were autistic, I would have found out about it previously." But I did start to wonder if I could have a diagnosis on the spectrum, even as I would waffle and tell myself "As long as Jody doesn't mention anything, it is all my imagination."

The day we finally did discuss my Aspie traits was the same day we held hands for the first time, on our walk up to the Royal Rosarian Gardens in Washington Park. There were actually three incidents that made this day a noteworthy day of transition. The first incident was when I had to stop at a store to use the restroom on our way. My small bladder can be rather annoying for me and anyone else traveling with me. Jody did not have any annoyance with me for the delay, and I was glad for that. His patience said something very positive about him. The second incident was our discussion about holding hands. I had been reading some weird stuff about autism, suggesting that Autistics don't like to be touched, not even to hold hands. I had wanted to ask Jody about this for a while, but I was nervous to ask him. I finally worked up the courage to inquire whether this is true or not, and I was relieved to hear that no, it is not true. Not only was I glad to hear that Jody would like to hold hands, I was even happier to discover that I could talk to him about it. The third incident was our discussion of my Aspie traits, because I was ready then to get Jody's feedback. I was ready to admit what I had noticed and start to consider the possibility of seeking diagnosis.

There were two other major influences on our relationship. The first of these was working together on various projects, from the presentation at Autscape to a painting we did together to poems that we wrote together by email. I enjoyed working together. I decided that I would like to work together for a career, keeping busy with a variety of activities. The second influence was Jody's circle of friends. As Jody introduced me to his friends, I felt welcomed and at ease with his circle. This was very important to me. It does not seem either sensible or kind to date someone if you dislike their friends; you would end up just tolerating them or not wanting your partner to spend time with them.

Conclusions and joint analysis

The discernment of when to transition your relationship from friendly acquaintance to something more deeply romantic is different for everyone. For Jody this discernment took a month. It began with the dating discussion at OHSU, with the knowledge that there was opportunity, followed by three pivotal dates (although other dates happened in between these): Valentine's Day, discussing Autscape; the movie day at Stacy's house, beginning the process of introducing Emilia to our friends; and the Rose Garden walk, introducing touch to our relationship. It was after this that Jody knew that he really wished to explore a romantic relationship, which for Jody meant he was seriously considering the possibility of marriage.

Emilia's journey of discernment took a different path, and was significantly longer. It started when she was a teenager, and lasted through the Rose Garden walk. Emilia did not think marriage was a possibility for herself for a number of years, which had a significant impact on her self-esteem. She did not feel she had the qualities that men were looking for in a wife. I (Emilia) told Jody that if we had met under similar circumstances a few years ago that we probably would not have gotten together. The experiences of the few years before we met were very important in mellowing and stabilizing my life. I had moved away from home and family, and being out on my own forced me to grow and change significantly. Because I was able to make it on my own (despite being told by some that I would not be able to) my confidence was dramatically increased.

The plot twists and turns

At this point you, the reader, are probably waiting for the analysis, the secret of dating. But, as we have said before, this does not exist. In the midst of our storytelling, we did not give a detailed plan as to how to ask someone on a date, or to court, for the reason that how you ask is purely individual, based on your unique circumstances. I (Jody) gave Emilia my contact information and said "if you're interested, give me a call." This put the ball in her court; would we go out or not? She asked and we did. When it came to hand-holding on 27 February

2006, she put the ball in my court, bringing up some research stating that Autistics do not like any kind of physical intimacy. Hearing this, I surmised that she had an interest in hand-holding and I initiated contact.

Someone has to take a risk to develop any relationship at any stage. In the end, it was about the timing. Everything lined up, a risk was taken, and it paid off. Timing is a key issue, sometimes more than what you say or how you say it, which will be discussed in greater detail in Chapter 6, as we look more into the transition from friendly acquaintance to romance, and in Chapter 7, when we look at the transition from romance to marriage.

Call to action

We have talked about taking time to make friends in the previous chapter, and in Chapter 3 we talked about engaging in activities in public with other people. However, what we haven't yet said is that another important thing is taking time for yourself, not because you have time that you need to waste, or because you did not get a date for Saturday night, but because you have scheduled an event for yourself that you enjoy doing. You need to maintain some time as an individual as you connect to a wider range of people. This is necessary in order to help you relax, regain composure, and to increase your abilities to contribute topics to conversations when you are with people because you will be able to talk about your solitary interests and events.

Your events could be walks, jumping out of an airplane, or eating a special treat by yourself with nobody else around. It does not matter what the activity is, as long as you enjoy it, and that it is legal, ethical, and moral. Both of us have activities that we do alone, and this rejuvenates us for our encounters with other people. Add to your dating plan a category for fun activities that you would prefer to do alone. Pick one and go do it. Write a journal that describes your experience. It could provide you with materials that you could present at an autism conference, or even put in a book that you write. Remember the call to action in Chapter 2: the next publication should be yours!

6. Encounters with Physical Intimacy

A garden off-season
Roses in Winter
Mizzled upon
Clipped short
They stem from the ground
They march in orderly rows
A backdrop for a peaceful walk together—weather permitting
Leafless, bare branches
Underneath tempered sky
Bereft of birdsong
A squirrel passes by
And high tails it home
We wonder about roses in winter
In the Royal Rosarian garden
In the lovely city of Portland
In the light of relational bliss
Meandering through hand in hand
Meticulously searching our thoughts
We say what comes to mind
Finding spring in winter
By Emilia and Jody, joint poem completed 4 March 2006

Being in close proximity, making eye-contact, hand-holding, linking arms, lap-sitting, hugging, kissing, tickling, massage, caressing, and/or any type of sex (digital, oral, vaginal, or anal) all fall under the broad umbrella of the term "physical intimacy." There are varying degrees of interest in any or all of these practices, and it is okay to engage in or to not engage in any of these practices under the right circumstances. Physical intimacy describes any activity that includes the intentional stimulus of the body for the purpose of generating pleasure of either or both participants. Stimulating another's body for the expressed purpose of pleasure is different from a handshake between friends, or a kiss of greetings or congratulation. Physical intimacy, in a romantic context, is a special way to open up to a person, and should not be engaged in casually.

The type of physical intimacy that you engage in will depend on a lot of factors: your spiritual tradition, your biological makeup, your sensory responses, your age, your experience level with physical intimacy, your desire for physical intimacy, geographic location, legal issues. Clearly, we cannot address every factor here, nor can we give a decent overview within the span of one chapter. Therefore, we thought it better to limit the number of subtopics, and cover a few things in depth. This chapter will address three issues specifically: desire, sensory issues, and personal meaning. These elements will apply to all individuals who attempt to engage in a relationship, and any improvement in these areas will serve to increase success in you relational endeavors.

Desire

Desire is the first point of address that we shall encounter. Some adults like to be touched, others do not. Some want firm touch, others soft. Some have extreme desires for sexual activity, and other adults have never felt any desire for sexual activity. All this is normal and people in all of these categories have developed very wonderful intimate relationships. They have communicated their desires to their partners, and have agreed on strategies to satisfy each of their unique desires. Specific intimacies (which one or the other may not have an interest or ability to engage in) don't have to create undue stresses on a relationship. Patience, creativity, and good communication can overcome challenges in this arena.

The expression of desire should always be confirmed by an expression of consent to intimate activity. Get the confirmation of consent, whether you have just met the person, have been dating them a long time, or even if you are married. Consent can be verbal or non-verbal, as long as both parties are aware that it is alright to proceed with engagement in the intimate expression. Unfortunately, consent does not always happen. In our call to action, we will discuss this further: what to do if you are being victimized, and what to do if someone accuses you of wrong-doing and you don't understand what you might have done.

Another aspect of desire is that it should not be a catalyst for guilt or shame. On the moral side of things, there are several religious traditions that have specific restrictions on a variety of intimate behaviors, but not necessarily upon your desires (a.k.a. your orientation). If you have sexual feelings both for people of the same gender as yourself and for people of the other gender, for example, and you choose to marry someone of the other gender, in many religions there would be no sin, and you would still have a sexual orientation that would not be classified as heterosexual.

However, if you have feelings for both genders and choose to engage sexually with someone of the same gender, you might place yourself in social jeopardy with your family and/or community, especially if your religious practice forbids this. Be very careful and try to foresee all the possible consequences of your actions if you do make this choice. Parents, family members, and friends, should not restrict your ability to find work, call you names, restrict your ability to find housing, humiliate you, violently attack you, etc., if you have a sexual practice that is in conflict with your family or community's religious beliefs. However, this does occur, and more often than you might think. Acting upon desire can have political and social consequences that one might have difficulty imagining. Be prepared!

Sensory issues

Sensory issues can be very challenging during the expression of physical intimacy. What romance novels, television shows, and movies portray about physical intimacy is often nowhere near the reality of romantic expression. For example, you often see a first kiss portrayed in the romance media as being exciting and highly pleasurable. However, we found our first kiss to be very awkward, and wondered why people found certain types of kissing to be pleasurable at all. We have since learned methods that have worked for us, and now enjoy kissing, but that took time and opportunity to get to know each other very well.

Sensory issues bring both strengths and strains to romance. In our Autscape presentation, and in presentations that have followed, we have presented a list to generate ideas from conference participants. We have found that with a little prompting, groups can generate a myriad of creative applications for sensory challenges in the realm of romantic relationships. Since touch is generally one of the most challenging to brainstorm, we include our comments here for your perusal and analysis.

Touch sensitivity

a. Strengths
    Increased possibility in picking up on unusual spasms
    and/or temperature levels in the significant other.

b. Strains
    Touch can be both a physical and an emotional intimacy,
    depending on how it is used. Until appropriate ways of
    dealing with touch defensiveness[1] are found, no matter
    what is said, the possibility still exists that touch
    defensiveness could be read as a rejection of the other. In
    most cases, the problem is *how* you are touched, not that you
    were touched.

If you have severe issues with touch, you might try finding a friend you know well and trust to engage in touch exploration. This worked

---

1   Touch defensiveness involves involuntary flinching, pulling away, or lashing out,
     generally caused by an unexpected touch, a touch during sensory overload, or a
     touch in an area that is normally hypersensitive.

very well for Jody. First you figure out what kinds of touch will not cause adverse reaction, then second, figure out what types of touch and/or cuddling will cause pleasure in all parties participating. Keep in mind that if you do try a touch exploration session, you need to be very careful. Most sexual violations occur with people who know you well, not with strangers. When doing a touch exploration make sure you have planned a way out, or have someone standing by in another room. The goal is to make these sessions clinical, something related to touch that is valuable for all who are participating, while protecting yourself in the process. We say this because eventually, if you engage in a series of touch exploration sessions, you may plan on doing a session where you take off some or all of your clothing to try skin to skin contact. This should not involve sex, just touch. If you are not an adult or if you are living with your parents or a caregiver, you should discuss touch exploration with them before engaging in the activity.

If you are an independent adult, talk to some trusted friends, a professional counselor, and/or a religious leader to gain some advice on how to proceed.

We do not have much wisdom to convey on this issue, but here are few points to ponder. First, decide on your goals *before* you try a touch exploration (e.g. lots of talking afterward, not having any romance), and when you try this, *do not* engage in sexual activity. This will be easier if, the first time you try this, you do not get completely naked. Second, decide what clothing items you are going to remove before you arrive at the location for your touch exploration session, and let the other person know what will happen. Make sure the other person responds in kind. Third, when trying new types of touch let the other know what is going to occur so they can be ready and agree *before* you start. Vary the amount of pressure used on different body parts, duration of contact, speed of caressing, etc., until you find out what works. The most important thing is to talk about what you did after you have finished and in the days that follow each encounter.

Touch is an intimacy, whether or not you plan on being romantic with the person you are exploring touch with. As casual and as clinical as you make these sessions, you will both still be emotionally vulnerable to a degree. It is important to treat the person you are relating with in a caring, respectful manner, letting that person know what is going on in your life, how you are feeling, and allowing that person to do the same with you. You want to reflect on what happened during your touch exploration session: what felt good, why it felt good, what those feelings meant in light of your friendship. Also, you want to check in periodically in the days that follow to see if new ideas about the session occurred.

We have provided quite a lot of information about touch exploration because we wished to include at least one sensory issue in-depth to demonstrate that there are ways to learn skills applicable to romantic relationships and circumvent challenges that arise. Some ideas would be less involved, such as not wearing perfume if your loved ones have olfactory sensitivities, or listening to music when your loved ones are not in the house if they have auditory sensitivities preventing the enjoyment of specific music genres or volume levels (e.g. listening to loud heavy metal).

Personal meaning

Personal meaning is something that includes desire, sensory issues, and a variety of other elements. For example, if you are a person who has never felt the desire for sexual intercourse, you will not find meaning when engaging in this practice. It does not mean that you will never have a wonderful, intimate relationship, because it is very possible to figure out ways that will work for you to be intimate. Do not believe people who say that you have not found the right person yet to bring out your sexual desire. You will never find the right person to bring out something in you that does not exist. If you have never felt sexual desire, you never will, and that is your orientation. This is not a new concept. Studies have been done on rodents and sheep suggesting there is a small percentage of these animals that do not mate. Also, asexuality was talked about in texts that date back thousands of years. One example from the Bible is:

> For there are some eunuchs, which were so born from their mother's womb: and there are some eunuchs, which were made eunuchs of men: and there be eunuchs, which have made them-

selves eunuchs for the kingdom of heaven's sake. He that is able
to receive it, let him receive it.

(Matthew 19:12, King James Version)

Don't worry about having sex if you have an asexual orientation. If
you want to establish a partnership with someone, try and seek out
another like yourself. However, if you choose to engage in a relationship with someone who has sexual desire, be upfront with them about
what type of physical expression has meaning for you. Find out what
has meaning for them and see if the possibility exists of finding a
compromise that works. Undoubtedly this is challenging, but people
have done it in the past, and will do so again in the future.

Now, for those who are sexually orientated, having sex can be a
fulfilling thing, emotionally and physically, under the right circumstances, just like other types of physical intimacy: hand-holding,
kissing, hugging, etc. If one is tending to the desires of the other, it
can hold personal meaning for both individuals, especially if you take
specific sensory issues into account. Physical intimacy can provide a
clear message to someone that you care for them, and be a powerful
symbol of commitment. It can also be very confusing, and, as a result,
thousands of books have been written on the subject. In other words,
we are not going to be able to explain all the mysteries of sex within a
few short pages. That is impossible.

In our stories for this chapter we aim to shed light on the fact that
two Autistics with similar religious practices, activity interests, ages,
and so on can view an act of physical intimacy in very different ways:

Jody's story

In the previous chapter I made reference to our Date in which Emilia
and I walked from Portland State University to the Royal Rosarian
Rose Garden in Washington Park. This was one of the final indicators
for me that it was okay to really open up more to Emilia and deepen
our relationship. We held hands for the first time on our way to the
park, and the holding of hands was an intense stimulus that I did not
expect.

In February I stopped trying to push our relationship along, and was looking for commonalities that suggested we were compatible. I was finding lots of these, and combined with the fact that Emilia was willing to look toward the future, and that she was starting to be introduced to my friends, the physical touch felt like the sealer of commitment, the handshake after the deal is struck. It was very powerful for me. I wanted to begin expressing myself physically with Emilia sooner, but I am very glad that we waited as long as we did to begin holding hands. It became an act of emotional intimacy, not just something physical.

In an email I sent her that night I talked about my head spinning (in a good way) and I started a poem via email that we wrote together (I sent a line, then she responded with a line) that we finished on 4 March 2006, influenced by our date. This poem is featured as the header for this chapter. We have also included more of our joint poetry wrting in Appendix A. Emilia's touch told me something special, and it was this personal meaning, more than anything else, that prompted my desires and gave me comfort in our journey as girl-friend and boyfriend.

Many factors were affecting our encounter. Part of what occurred on our rose garden walk was emotional, but there was a significant part that was also physical. It was raining slightly that day, not the moment when we left on our walk, but as the day progressed. It was slightly cooler, due to the wind chill, which enhanced the warmth felt with our hands together. Heat, combined with a little coolness, can be a boost of fun.

As the date progressed, it started to rain a little harder, so we decided to head back to the university. We were getting wet and as we were wandering around a bend in the road, we came upon a set of playground equipment (slides, ladders, etc.). We chatted under this equipment for a few minutes, then continued on. Our misadventure in the rain became a bonding force, a small difficulty faced together. I had a wonderful time. Emilia did too.

On 29 May 2007, in the middle of a visit of my in-laws from the state of Montana, we decided to go for a walk in the rose garden, Emilia's parents and us. I related that experience to my mother-in-law, and it felt like I shared something very intimate. It was a conversation that took place as Emilia and her dad walked away to look at some flowers on the other side of the garden, and her mother wanted to rest. I stayed with her and we chatted. It was good to share something personal at that point, and it reminded me that the rainy day at the gardens was one of the best dates Emilia and I had ever had.

In other words, the stimulus created by Emilia, with emotional as well as physical connection, created a stimulus only achievable with her. Others can be brought close through the sharing of that event, but it is the event itself that, in a metaphorical sense, becomes the center of the earthly universe. I still pick at my lips, flap, jump up and down, and rub the sides of my chest, but I can do that anywhere. These self-stimulatory behaviors serve a purpose that is healthy in my life. However, Emilia provides me with something more, when we are looking at my life from an autism perspective. She provides even more as a team-mate in our quest to change the world for the better, and in our quest to maintain a happy and functional home.

Emilia's story

As a young person, I discovered naughty romantic fiction, and found it to be rather fascinating. I wondered about the sexual activities that the characters engaged in, and had an intense theoretical interest. The characters seemed to derive such pleasure from their sexual encounters, which were described in great detail. I say that my interest was theoretical because I didn't feel an attraction to or passion for the guys I saw around school. They tended to make me nervous, or if not, they were like family to me.

Several times, I went out on one or two dates with a guy, but didn't find him sexually attractive. I would admire his good-natured qualities, but couldn't imagine wanting him to touch me. One would seem too much like a cousin, another would be like a brother. I would never go out with a guy more than twice if I felt that way; I thought that it would be unfair to him. My mother had always said "If you don't date someone, you won't marry him." I considered passion to be an important element of marriage, and would not have wanted to marry without it. In hindsight I can see that I was really putting too much importance on that physical element. I also lacked patience, and did not realize that such things may need to develop over time.

As I got to know and trust Jody, I gained more appreciation for all of him—from his keen mind, to his kind heart, to his nicely shaped body. I was a little bit surprised and very happy to find that my theoretical interest in sexuality turned into directed interest when Jody and I started to hold hands. It was a confirmation for me that we would be a good team. I wanted to share all my life with my life partner, not just part of it. I wanted to work together, play together, pray together, and make love together. I could tell from holding hands that Jody was gentle and sensitive, two qualities that I thought would be essential in a lover.

In my opinion, the most important thing for enjoying physical intimacy is to ignore the image put out in the media (both books and movies). Much of the romantic fiction put out for mass consumption is really pornography for women, and like all pornography, it is not good or healthy. The sexual side of relationships is emphasized completely beyond proportion, while other important relational aspects are completely neglected. Unrealistic expectations formed from these sources can spoil something that would otherwise be a lovely experience. At the beginning of our marriage, I struggled with my expectations. I inflicted much stress and unhappiness upon myself that was completely unnecessary. I needed to relax and enjoy our physicality (which I very much do now). Our physical expression of love for each other has added to our partnership in several ways. It has been a way to show affection, to comfort, and to relax. It is something special that we share only with each other.

Conclusion and joint analysis

In this chapter, like in others, we have spoken about issues related to timing. When do you engage in a specific action during the course of a relationship to make the action more effective? This is still the key question. Physical intimacies should be expressed when both parties are willing to engage in them, which in many places is subject to legal definition with punishment for any violations defined under local law. For example, if you have sex with someone when they do not want it, you can be imprisoned in several countries, or even killed, depending on what part of the world you are residing in. Even if you are just visiting in that part of the world, you are still subject to the legal definitions of the location where you are, no matter your country of origin.

Also related to timing is the use of pornography. Many young people, both male and female get into the use of pornography out of a natural curiosity to explore sexuality. As demonstrated by Emilia's story, some of your more intense romances can be used by the female population as a means to excite interests in sexual passions. However, if you are very young and engaging in this behavior, you might not fully understand that these stories are not based in reality, just as the pornographic materials that are marketed to males are not based in reality. In some ways female pornography can be even more disastrous, if the consumer has read a lot of fairy tales in her youth that contain the stereotypical "prince saves the girl in distress" with a passionate kiss at the end. Parents should think about the messages that are sent to their kids in the literature that they consume, right from the time they are infants, because kids, disabled or not, grow up and remember many of the lessons that were taught to them from their parents, and the media that they were exposed to.

On the positive side, when taking action and expressing your desires in a legal, moral and ethical manner, you open yourself up the possibility of developing your relationship in ways that are fantastic and beyond comprehension. This desire-connection was clarified for us when we had a positive relational experience (when we got together). We understand so much more now, but even with our new understanding, much of our relationship is still beyond our comprehension, and we still live with this every day as husband and wife.

One of the more challenging things to understand is that a date can be less than perfect and yet be better than something that has gone smoothly. When Jody mentioned the rain and the cold, along with huddling under some playground equipment, this was positive in a romantic context. Adversity, challenge, and/or stress is not always a binding force in a relationship, but it can be. Don't plan on difficulty in the relationship, but if it does happen, whether it is rain on a walk, bad food at a restaurant, or something really horrible, do not think that your relationship is through because you had one bad date by your planning standards. You might have an intense emotional moment and find it was one of the coolest events in your life.

There are differences regarding how people experience the same physical intimacies, as evidenced by our stories of hand-holding, and that is okay. Talk about your experiences with your significant other, and see what new insights you can gain. Each passing day can be a treasure-trove of new discovery.

Note for parents and caregivers

Sex is a scary thing for parents and caregivers of people with and without disabilities. There is a continuum of scariness, from completely scary to not scary at all. Unfortunately, for those with disabled offspring, sometimes sex continues to move toward the completely scary end of the spectrum. This should not be the case. It is natural for people to develop an interest in their bodies, whether or not they are disabled. If they are disabled, it is very important they get a strong sex education, starting very young, because of the high amount of sexual abuse that occurs. Unfortunately, some caregivers and/or family members, as well as strangers, take advantage of a situation and do inappropriate things with people, causing much stress for the victim.

High stress means less talking for a lot of Autistics, which unfortunately means that Autistics become a vulnerable target. Providing tools to make sense of inappropriate sexual behaviors reduces the chances for victimization. It also reduces the possibility that an Autistic will be accused of inappropriate acting out of sexual desire.

Methods for caregivers to impart sex education to Autistics, both the positive sides and the negative, are wide open for creative application. Everyone interprets information in widely different ways. Some will be oriented to the spoken word, some the written word, pictures, tactile input—a merry mix. Do what works best for the person under your charge. Go at a pace that is suitable for him and do not feel constrained by a sex education program that you read out of a book, read online, or receive at a conference. Good education is individual and flexible. You know the Autistic in your life better than anyone else does.

Call to action

As promised in the section on desire, we are including information regarding what to do if you are being victimized, or if someone is accusing you of being a victimizer, socially or sexually. We include this because we have met several Autistics who were not aware that specific behaviors directed toward them were unhealthy and illegal. They only knew they did not like those behaviors.

In response to their disclosure, we imparted some strategies to avoid these issues in the future. We feel very passionate about people who are stuck in situations like these. We have seen too many potential relationships in our circle of friends and associates that have been devastated by sexual deviance, and we hope to help reduce it through some basic social education, to avoid future pain and suffering for as many people as possible.

If the behavior of someone in your life is considered by others to be harassment, stalking, intimidation, rape, brutality or humiliation ask the people who are saying this why they believe it to be so. Then consider this evidence that you might be a victim of abuse. Abuse is not your fault. You deserve to be treated well and you should not tolerate abusive behavior. You need to tell the offending party to stop and/or act upon the knowledge of your abuse with the appropriate authorities. If you do not know the appropriate authority, you need to ask someone who is good with people to help you—specifically, someone you already trust. A police officer or a priest can also be a good choice for assistance. Most police officers and priests are trustworthy. However, if you are abused by a police officer or priest, go to another precinct or parish, and report the abuse, so that the abuser can be removed from his position of authority. If the person you tell does not do something in response to your disclosure, keep telling people till the offensive behavior is stopped.

If you hear words like harassment, stalking, or intimidation used to describe your behavior toward someone else, ask someone you trust (not the person who is describing your behavior as abusive) to explain what is going on. I (Jody) had to do this when I was younger. I was trying to get to know another individual and did not understand there was a problem. If you don't know a trustworthy person who has good people skills, you might ask a priest, a police officer, or a lawyer. (Unfortunately, lawyers tend to charge a lot of money for a consultation, so in this case speaking to a lawyer should be a last resort, unless they are a close personal friend.)

If someone has identified your behavior as harassment, stalking, or intimidation, it is important to determine whether or not you should continue your attempts at relating to that person. Some situations might be a simple misunderstanding of a facial expression or something you said, and in that case a brief explanation or an apology might solve the problem (coinciding with a plan to change the offending action). Unfortunately, some individuals might be so disturbed by your behavior that any attempts to fix the relationship will make the situation more stressful than it already is. Autistics need to seek out advice from time to time to check their behaviors to see if it is appropriate. This is normal, healthy, and something that should be done if you hear words like harassment, stalking, or intimidation referring to your behavior, even if you were not intending to engage in any of these practices. (Note: non-Autistics have issues in this area from time to time, just like Autistics.)

It's important to realize that, if you are not Autistic and feel that an Autistic is harassing, stalking, or intimidating you, this may not be intentional on their part. The biggest favor you can do for the individual is to be upfront and honest with this person. Blunt is better. Many Autistics do not understand hints, "the look," or non-tangible emotion-laden terms. Autistics have feelings, and are aware of them, but many have difficulty expressing them in the same words that non-Autistics use, even if they are labeled with "high-functioning Autism" or "Asperger's Syndrome."

If you are a family member or a caregiver of an Autistic and someone has described a specific behavior of theirs as being abusive, all of these comments made so far apply to you too. Describe to the Autistic the tangible behavior that is causing trouble, and why it is causing trouble. It could be a simple misunderstanding, or it might be something more serious. In any case, you might be in a position to explain what can be done to change the offending behavior to a positive outcome, saving a lot of stress and anxiety for all parties involved.

7. Moving Toward Marriage or Other Types of Long-Term Commitment

Love Song
Warming thoughts and feelings sire
Holding you is my desire
Hand in hand we could acquire
A loving bond tonight

Magic mouthful merrily
Scalding tongue topography
Untamed nights just you and me
Laughing dance and play

Lady dancer wafting pyre
Pallid thoughts in mind prefire
I'll sing you songs and I'll strum the lyre
A self-made man tonight

(Repeat)

Will you be my wife
Oh lady, for the rest of my life

By Jody John Ramey (2006)

We thought that meeting a potential romantic partner and going from friendly acquaintance to dating were gigantic hurdles. However, the engagement period was just as large a hurdle for us. For many couples in the United States, engagement is more like courting than like dating. Family and friends are more involved in the relationship, and in general your status as a couple is taken more seriously. Since we "dorted," "dated with greater elements of courting," this was not a huge change for us in that regard, but we still needed to plan the wedding, go to pre-marital counseling sessions at the church, figure out where we were going to live, plan how we were going to pay our bills, plan how we were going to deal with school, etc. We were also planning on a trip to Bozeman, Montana, USA, to see the stomping ground of Emilia's youth.

This trip was very important in our marriage process. Before we got engaged, we decided that it was important for each of us to have a tour of the places where the other grew up—to connect names to places, to faces—and since I (Jody) was born in Vancouver, Washington, USA, a 15-minute drive north from Portland, we only had to travel a far distance to visit Emilia's youthful stomping ground. The important aspect in this scenario was the travel, because through this not only did we get a deeper understanding of each other by having a common experience of the space itself, but we saw each other in an atmosphere of intense flowering.

Travel brings out things in individuals you do not see every day. While traveling, you see your traveling companion stressed, tired, confused or unprepared. Many individuals have reported that by traveling a significant distance with a person, they have either cemented their relationship, or ended it. With us, obviously, the trip was a good thing. We stayed with Emilia's parents just north of Bozeman, and drove almost daily into town. One day we went to Belgrade, where Emilia's brother and sister-in-law live. This was not the first time that I (Jody) had met them, but it was the first time I saw them in their homes, rather than in Portland, Oregon, USA, in an atmosphere where they were visiting us. There was one day during that trip that we, along with Emilia's parents, traveled to Yellowstone National Park across the border in Wyoming. (That was loads of fun, especially when the car was surrounded by buffalo. They made a most unique low grunting sound, and the buffalo babies were very cute.)

We received the blessings of both of our parents before we proceeded with the process of getting married. We thought this was very important, insomuch as our parents have known us all our lives. Parents often have a good idea of their children's strengths and weaknesses, and have insight on what sort of person each of their children would be compatible with. Many people who are courting have already experienced this, since they have probably had their parents involved from the beginning, but we encourage those of you who date, especially younger couples (under 40), to seek out parental advice early in your relationship. We did not wait to get engaged before we made first contact with our parents, and we hope you don't either (assuming that the relationship with your parents is a healthy one).

Transitioning to marriage, co-habitation, marriage, or other alternative forms of extended, committed relationships, like transitioning from friendly acquaintance to romance, is a change of intimacy —a time of opening yourself up even more to the one you intend to spend your life with. Issues of family planning including sensory hypersensitivities. (For example, Emilia has hypersensitive hearing, and screaming children often hurt her ears. Part of family planning for her is finding solutions to noise problems), rights and responsibilities of parenting, financial issues and others will need to be addressed in light of your potential responsibilities in these matters. If these and other topics are not discussed in detail, your relationship after you get married will suffer additional strains.

After the wedding, the relationship really becomes intimate, and issues such as snoring, bathing, bathroom habits, etc., come to the surface very fast. You won't wish to compound this with questions such as, "Do you want kids?", or "What faith should we raise them in?" We were very glad that we were required by the Catholic Church to do some pre-marital counseling, and found their methods very valuable. First, we did a Marriage Focus Inventory (Foccus 2000), which was a 156-question instrument that tested values and ideals across a range of areas. When we started the counseling sessions (a.k.a. "marriage prep classes"), we talked about areas of disagreement in our answers. We agreed in a lot of areas, and in most of the areas where we disagreed it was because we did not understand the questions properly. We also covered topics in counseling that we simply hadn't talked about yet. The inventory revealed that we really had not discussed financial planning, and so we had several sessions with the pastoral associate in which these topics were addressed, along with a couple of other topics.

Of course, there were many elements that affected how our relationship evolved over time, including our family backgrounds, our circles of friends, and even our education. In the next two paragraphs, Jody will share thoughts on relationships that he has gleaned from his time at university.

To begin a relationship, one needs to have something to offer, and a reason to do so. The person receiving the offer needs to have something to give back to continue the encounter, and if the initiator of the relationship does not want to receive what is offered back, the relationship might end there too. We are not talking about money, or tangible goods for barter, we are talking about social capital, and specifically, social capital as it applies to romantic relationships. Social capital is a concept in business, economics, political science, and sociology. Definitions vary from discipline to discipline, but generally, academics recognize that there are advantages created by positive connections to other people. These connections assist people in gaining more success in particular relational settings.

From the beginning of our relationship, from meeting each other on 10 September 2005, to becoming friendly acquaintances, to becoming romantically involved, to our transition into marriage, there were a multitude of times that we could have gone our separate ways. However, each of us demonstrated enough social resources to satisfy the needs of the other—social capital in action. How social capital pays off, scores a bit differently during each successive step in the romance process, and it is here that we see the conclusion of dating—or do we…?

Jody's story

I decided to tell one story in this book in a style of my personal thought process, to show a little of my Autistic side. Some people at conferences question that I am Autistic, because I can go for short periods showing almost no traits that would indicate my diagnosable qualities. However, I cannot do this for more than a short time. Yes, I am successfully married, after getting a Master's degree. I have been employed, but as of writing this paragraph, I am in the process of looking for work, after several months of being unemployed. I am real. I is who I is; that is all who I will be.

The mind thinks: Streams of thinking from the past, in the present, about the future, presented in words and word pictures

I think of my romantic relationship as a performance. My wife does not know that I love her. I must perform love, in a way that is believable. My non-verbal signals must match the verbal signals. From day one I presented my stock character to her, and she enjoyed my performance. Now, in my role as a man preparing to take the plunge into marriage, I must play the responsible planner. What I have said and how I have said it has depended on the context, which was influenced by my social environment, biologic makeup, geography, and personal impulse. A person's response serves to create a social situation that further shapes your language output. Even the biological transformations you experience during the ageing process will elicit in a change in people's response to you as an individual. This may seem large, frightening and overwhelming. However, a basic understanding that there is a linguistic system is necessary as we seek friends and romantic partners.

I was seeking at the beginning of my relationship with Emilia, than I was at a stage of discovering. When planning the wedding, the honeymoon, the place to live, how the bills are to be paid—all this and more—I had to make sure it all matches up, what I said and did. It makes me glad that I did not apply much of the stuff that a lot of the dating books put forth, because I cannot keep up that kind of lying. I am who I am, and I must behave as such, through the dating process, through the engagement, and even after the wedding. I am a successful man because I keep the relationship in an area in which I can converse, make plans. I create the world in which I live and I am a success.

I am a success, and it has been hard to function in a world in which people tell me I am wrong all the time, and to create a world on my terms in which to live. How can I be right and other people be wrong. Everyone says my relationship is right, but the rest of me is wrong. Are they right? Only about the relationship? I am good too. My behavior is appropriate, even though it is not appropriate at times. There is a constant dialog, sometimes filled with doubt, sometimes filled with anger and disgust, not at the woman who is now my wife, but at the world that is rotting away. I do not like my society. I get depressed, but I try and cheer up for the blessing in my life. I love my wife. I loved her when we got engaged, I love her more every day. I knew the timing of when to ask Emilia, because we had been talking about the possibility of marriage, what to do.

Autistics Are Awesome

STRONG FOCUS

Ability to focus on one objective paves the way toward
accomplishing large and challenging tasks.

INDEPENDENT THINKING

Ability to consider unpopular or unusual possibilities generates new opportunities for others.

ATTENTION TO DETAIL

Ability to remember and process minute details creates a solid foundation to solve complex issues.

Lovely + Loving + Loveable

Transferring my life from single-hood to marriage-dom was a tumultuous experience. It was fun, stressful, and I thank my creator often that it happened. No, I do not wish to do it again, but if I went back in time and was given the opportunity to re-choose my path, I would choose it again. However, if given the opportunity to tell my story again, I might choose a different path.

This has been a very personal revelation in this chapter, which I hope you readers will appreciate. What you saw in my story was a thought process similar to what goes on in my head, what went on during the time I was engaged. I chose not to translate for you. My thinking process is associative, not linear and it might confuse you if you do not think in the exact same way as I do.

Yet, I will provide some explanation.

I think of love as a performance. When I say things that people consider "sensitive," give a gift, or show with my body language that I am listening to another person as they relay some challenging aspect of their life, I am putting on a show. I am loving them, but I might be concentrating on the outward signs a little more than the average person. There was a definite switch from behaving in dating mode, to behaving in marriage mode, with the social expectations of these two distinct aspects of living, but in this transition, it was important to maintain myself as who I am, as an Autistic, because I cannot maintain facades for very long. There is a distinct pressure to bend to society, which I experienced during the transition into marriage, but I am thankful that I resisted the urge to bend to those external forces. Many disabled people are raised to think that the non-disabled viewpoint is always the correct one, but to follow that as a disabled person, especially in matters of love, can be the cause of extreme difficultly.

Emilia's story

When composing the "Emilia's story" sections of this book, putting my thoughts down on paper was not the easiest thing in the world to do. Often Jody and I would discuss the story that I was writing. I would tell him about it and he might ask me questions to clarify. Then he would say, "That's it, write that." I would reply "Write what?," and my head would feel empty, as if all the things I had just been talking about had disappeared.

Working together has been a part of our relationship from the beginning, and that work has been communicative, from our first major project (our dating presentation at Autscape 2006) to our most recent (the manuscript for this book). Jody and I are a team. When did we meet? At the right time. I liked the direction Jody was going in, and seemed to be able to join in with his help. He guided me in my areas of weakness and expressed his appreciation for the help that I could give him. Naturally we all have areas where we need a little "fine tuning," and our cooperation has been really nice.

Communicating is not necessarily easy for me, whether it is in person or in written form, but I have made progress in my communication. Early on in our relationship, I would become very stressed when having to address a number of subjects. Jody helped me to face things that I had been afraid to talk about with anyone before (I would even avoid thinking about them) and that gave me confidence in our future as a married couple. I knew that I could trust him, and that was very important to me. It is not that we have perfected our communication, but we are learning.

I have learned to not make assumptions. If Jody says something and I start to take offense, I ask him what he means by what he has said. For example, I was offended when I asked my husband a question and he replied "whatever." I thought he was being sarcastic. I asked him, and it turns out that when he says "whatever" it means "OK" or "that's fine." If I hadn't asked him, I could have become resentful toward him over a simple misunderstanding. We use words in different ways. For Jody, a "snack" and a "snackie" is the same thing, whereas for me, it is completely different. (Because of a long-running joke between us, to me a snack is edible, and a snackie is something one would not eat.) The important thing is that we communicate as clearly as we can. When I don't understand something, I ask for clarification. If I start to feel offended, or if my feelings are hurt, I don't assume that Jody intends that result with his words.

Through our joint poetry writing and his impromptu songs, I have developed an appreciation of Jody's use of language. He relates to me on multiple levels and in multiple dimensions with his language.

Language has always been important to me. I like words that sound similar, or have auditory connections to each other. I find such words, and then find ways to connect them with story or poem. I notice the distinctive differences between similar sounding words of different languages, and it matters to me. The structure of language is fascinating, and the time I spent learning something about linguistics at Portland State University was a wonderful time of discovery, an adventure.

Conclusions and joint analysis

After reading these stories one might assume that Emilia is an auditory thinker, based upon her words, "I like words that sound similar, or have auditory connections to each other. I find such words, and then find ways to connect them with story or poem." One might find the thought process of Jody more visual, based upon the word picture "Autistics are Awesome." However, neither are completely true. Emilia is auditory but also very connected to her visual channel, whereas Jody relies very little on visual information; Jody is more kin-esthetic and olfactory in his thinking.[1]

Communication for us, and for many Autistics is a matter of translation and re-translation and re-re-translation. We have our thought process, then we translate to the language of communication being used (English), then translate it again to the mode of impartation (in our case this book you are reading). There are, of course, more steps but we are simplifying for the sake of brevity.

We applied "re-re-re-translation" to the writing of the manuscript for the book you're reading, and to the relationship that we are continuing to build.

---

1   Kinesthetic thought is based in motion; olfactory thought is based on scent.

Dating does not end after you get married. Some of our goals have changed in the dating process, but the art of trying to learn about each other, the creative ways to impress and please the other, in many ways have retained their form. We have continued many of the same discussions, and taken them to a new level, but the work does not end. Meeting someone is work, becoming friends is work, transitioning friendship and/or friendly acquaintances to a romantic relationship (dating/courting to engagement, to marriage) requires work. Some people describe love in a linguistic way, saying that love is not a noun, that it is an action verb. Either way, it is not easy, but it can be a lot of fun.

We will go on to say more about this in our closing remarks to this book.

Note to parents and caregivers

If you are a parent or caregiver of someone who is quite visibly Autistic, we are glad you have read this far. Many parents look at their non-verbal children who scream, throw tantrums, bite themselves and/or others and do not think that they will grow up to earn a graduate degree and/or get married. However, we have met Autistics who have started talking as late as the age of 12 who have done just that. They may be the exceptions to the rule, but there are always possibilities, and you do not know how they are going to present themselves.

It is also conceivable, even if the Autistic under your charge does not have huge success with education, that he[2] still might want get married, especially if he is allowed to date. How do you proceed if you are a caregiver and you know that your charge is not able to run a household by himself? Simple. You find out if he understands what a marital relationship is, what sex is, what the results of engaging in sex are, and then you start planning on appropriate resources and supports that might be available over the short and long term, making sure that the marriage is feasible before it happens. You

2   Again, we are using the generic "he" to avoid the awkward "he/she."

also provide education to fill in specific knowledge gaps, whether or not the marriage is currently feasible. Things could change in the future.

We have met several couples where one or both participants in the relationship had intellectual disabilities that were quite noticeable. They did not run their households by themselves. Nobody now in the western world really does. Think about it. When getting stressed about issues in life that come up, you talk to people to get advice. When moving from one home to another, many people get help in the process. Non-disabled people have help in maintaining their marriages all the time, and so should people who have disabilities.

Find out what resources are in your community for the Autistics in your life. They could be churches, community centers, non-governmental/ non-profit organizations, etc. Are there people who can assist with financial management, household chores, emotional guidance, etc.? Are there people in your own family that can provide such support? We say people, because there really should be more than one person involved, from more than one household. If you as a parent are doing all the support activities, you need to consider what will happen to your children if something happens to you.

Call to action

The call to action in each chapter has not been intended to be a separate call, but rather, several pieces to one large call to action, sharing yourself in a positive way with your community. This sharing can include participating in activities that you like as an individual, with friends, with romantic partners, and more. Each separate call to action is an interlink to build this web of connection for you, to present a positive message of Autistic success to those around you. We believe that success is not independence, but societal interdependence. This applies to people with and without disabilities. Even if you do not wish to present at a conference, write an article, or a book, you can still volunteer together with your significant other to help the community in which you live. This is our final call to action and we want to say in it that when you find someone to be romantic with, volunteer with an organization in your community, or on a cause that will be helpful in some way—one that is visible to others. (Of course, you do not need to wait until you find someone to volunteer, and may even find volunteer work to be a good way to meet potential friends and romantic partners.)

Volunteering could be in your church, for a non-governmental organization/non-profit organization, a neighborhood association—any positive thing that you and your significant other would both enjoy doing. It will get you working together, and demonstrate to those who see you that Autistics are valuable to society, and that Autistics can have positive romantic relationships with each other (which is positive publicity for our kind). This activity does not need to be all-consuming of your time, and can even be a once-per-month affair. Emilia and I have enjoyed working together as much as we have enjoyed playing together. There are differences in the types of pleasure received, but we have found that both are valuable to our relationship.

Closing remarks

We mentioned earlier that after getting married, we are still dating. Part of this means we are still trying to impress each other, learning more about each other, going to new places, trying new activities, etc. We have even learned a few skills that would probably have been helpful in the romantic process before marriage: how to derive pleasure from each other's special interests when we do not share in that special interest. This may seem challenging at first, but it can be quite fun, and it is helpful in other relationships, not just romantic ones.

When engaging in someone else's special interest, you pay attention to what the interest is, and try to find an aspect of it that is fascinating for you. For example, I, Jody, have an interest in Antarctica that Emilia does not share. Emilia decided that she found penguins interesting, and the lava lake in Mount Erebus, and she can direct conversations toward those topics when I am passionate about Antarctica.

If there is not an aspect of the topic you find interesting, there are other options. I (Emilia) have a passionate interest in the harp. I can listen to harp music for hours, read about the harp, and my family and friends got together and gave me a harp as a birthday gift, so now I can learn how to play. Jody does not seem very interested in the harp at this point, but he does seem to find my fascination with the harp to be fascinating. He likes to see my enthusiasm and happiness when I am obsessing on the harp. Whatever your hook for the other's interest is, go with it, as long as it is legal, ethical and moral. Have fun with your partner on many levels, for it is fun that can make life worth living.

Appendix A:
Interactive Poetry

One of the wonderful interactive activities we engaged in during the course of our dating relationship, before we got married, was writing poetry. We did not do this in a manner that most people would imagine. Even though we lived near each other, and saw each other almost every day, we would write via email. One of us would start a poem, then the other would add, subtract, edit, or rearrange a bit and send it back, and this would continue till we both said it was complete.

The header for Chapter 6 was one of our tandem poems, which we composed about a stroll through the Royal Rosarian Rose Garden in Portland, OR, USA. As our relationship progressed, the imagery for our poems continued to be drawn from our experiences. Earlier on, the poetry we had composed was based upon literary and cultural references. However, the earlier poems became sources to draw upon, as we developed our restricted code of communication. We have included a sample here for your perusal, to see how our style progressed over a couple of months.

The first poem was our initial joint composition, and was not based on a common experience. Even after being married for a year, we still occasionally make reference to images described in this poem in our personal conversation. The second poem was based upon some rainy-day walks we had, and the third poem was based upon a date at the Pioneer Place Mall. We wandered around and ended up in an electronics store, where we watched an advertisement movie that was very loud, and did not sit too well with our hypersensitivities.

We do not keep to rigid rhyme schemes or poetic models. Our poems are not great art. Rather, they are artefacts from an earlier stage in our relationship. If you choose to engage in this type of poetry writing, do not restrict yourself to mere quality of art. Instead, look at the art of human relationship. It is this art that provides the greatest inspiration for all other arts to draw upon.

From the Tub to the Heavens (e.g. water baptism)

People occasionally ponder
Questioning all that is
Understanding little
Of what life has to offer
This day I number among those
Sitting in my own bathtub
Fully clothed
Very soon to be soaked by a rising tide
Just as a year ago, when on the beach
Same clothing, same bare feet
It's captivating, scintillating, it's highly natural
This flowing lava that approaches my form
I am a mountain, in a range forlorn
Kindle in me a fire
I say to my creator
Xanthochroid in my perception
Does Jesus continue to get whiter with every passing year
Would a Jewish man wandering the desert be an angry
WASP
Judging?
Hateful?
Many Churches portray him as such, but why?
Then come the words of Psalm 23:
The L-rd[1] is my Shepherd; I shall not want.

---

1   Many Jews and Messianic believers spell L-rd and G-d without the "o" in fulfillment of the commandment "Thou shalt not take the name of the L-rd G-d in vain." If the paper these words were written on was destroyed, you would not be desecrating the name of your creator.

He maketh me to lie down in green pastures:
He leadeth me beside the still waters.
He restoreth my soul: he leadeth me
In the paths of righteousness
For his name's sake[2]
Heated fluid envelops my toes
Dancing slowly in sync
With some unheard melody
Heading upstream
To create a zany conglomeration
Of human, textile and water
A new garnish for this event
A warm night in the sun
A cool day beneath the moon
Laying down I look at the stars
Twinkling from some distant galaxy
Daft people pour into my tub
With a time bomb, and a keg of beer
It is a time to party, a time to fear
But I need a time of peace
Once in a While
Zion's successor will rule this gathering human infestation
The xenomorphic personalities that distract me at times
Attempting to lead me astray
But as I travel a few more steps
Down the yellow brick road
To a seismic yellow submarine
I quietly consider the universe
With its vast spaces
Places untouched by questions
I am awestruck, rejuvenated, reborn
Seeing the light of The L-rd
And my clothes are dripping wet

By Emilia and Jody, poem completed on 12 February 2006

2   King James Version.

Springtime in Portland

Today the sun
Cannot be seen
We run among
The soggy leaves
Wet with rain
And when the day's
Last light is gone
We stop to pray
And ask for peace
We place our ways
In the hands of him
Who founded love
With confident trust
That our new-found love
Is in his care

By Emilia and Jody, poem completed on 25 March 2006

What's Next?

Unfortunately there are times and seasons
When the death-sucking core machine
Permeates your inner sanctum
It is good to depart this realm of the machine
To indulge the fantasy of being elsewhere
Positively pugnacious, feelings free from strife
There are times when you might sit
In the Pioneer Place Mall in
Portland, Oregon
Expecting to briefly relax
In a dim, comfortable place
Pondering a small theater of ads
Then you are aurally bombarded
Feeling pain, hearing echoes
Plundering your inner securities
We left that place, that secluded theater
In the back of some no-name store

Positively out of reach of our current finances
We saved the day, the date, daintily, disconcerted
Yet enraptured by the closeness we felt in the moment
Poetry to illustrate the depth of human romance
Desire eats away hunger, and there is a certain
indulgence
In the pleasure that is present in both beings of this
relational union
Pressing fortune against fortune as they walk through
the mall
Happiness, peace, questioning, healing
Death-sucking machine at rest
Post-mortem in the USA.

By Emilia and Jody, poem completed on 11 April 2006

Appendix B:
Perspectives in Perspective

Emilia's perspective

This word picture (see below) came from an exercise to find words that might go well together in a poem. I began the process with a word. Then I added words to the first, each with a slight change. The related words are arranged to show visually the sound connections

<pre>
              wheat
                meet   team
    night   might   time
                mate   tame
          moat   tome   note
  boat   moot   tone
      boot   tomb
</pre>

"Word picture," by Emilia Murry Ramey

between them. Starting with team, there is a curving line of words—each one has been changed by one phoneme (sound) from the word before. Then each word is paired across with a word that is its mirror opposite (in sound, not spelling: might and time, for example). The paired words make the foundation of the word picture, and the additional words branch off from the main lines.

Not all of the words in this picture relate to each other, but it is interesting to find connections between them. "Tame" and "mate" remind me of the play *Taming of the Shrew*. "Night," "time," "moat," "boat," and "wheat" could all have come out of a mystery story about a castle. The lines of words were put together to form nice lines, but without any thought to represent a particular letter or symbol. I'd like to try working toward a picture or symbol or letter with the arrangement of words. On the other hand, it would be fun to try a theme, and see how many related words I could work into a design.

Jody's perspective

I see a picture. I know there are words, but they hold no meaning, no connection as words to other words, words to stories, or words in their individuality. The shape that the words make, as a whole, might be a letter from a language that I do not speak. The shape may be a waveform measuring the energy of sound. The shape might also be a signature stamp. When reading the words individually, I cannot see what the words represent. I know what a note, is, a tone, time. I'm a musician. Yet I still cannot see the notes, tones, time, etc., in this picture, because this is a visual context for the words to me. They are strokes of paint. Emilia sees these words differently, but I am incapable of doing so at the time of writing this paragraph, even though she has explained her process of constructing the word picture to me.

However, the fact that Emilia sees a very different picture than I do does not bother me. It reassures me that, despite the multi-layered interconnectedness that we experience in our relationship, that there are aspects of her that I will continue to get to know over the years, and that there are strengths in her that I do not have. I see separateness when I look at this picture, because Emilia sees something that I cannot, but I also see a profound depth of power, not only emanating from Emilia, but from my creator through Emilia, because we are matched so well, with interlacing strengths and weaknesses, and a desire to make our union sacred, as the precepts of our faith practice define.

References

Edmonds, G. and Worton, D. (2005) *The Asperger Love Guide: A Practical Guide for Adults with Asperger's Syndrome to Seeking and Maintaining Successful Relationships.* London: Sage Publications Ltd.

Foccus (2000) *Facilitating Open Couple Communication, Understanding & Study, Catholic edition.* Omaha, NE: Foccus Inc.

Lawson, W. (2005) *Sex, Sexuality and the Autism Spectrum.* London: Jessica Kingsley Publishers.

Newport, J. and Newport, M. (2002) *Autism-Asperger's and Sexuality: Puberty and Beyond.* Arlington, TX: Future Horizons.

Slater-Walker, C. and Slater-Walker, G. (2002) *An Asperger Marriage.* London: Jessica Kingsley Publishers.

Stanford, A. (2002) *Asperger Syndrome and Long-Term Relationships.* London: Jessica Kingsley Publishers.

St. Denis, R. (1939) An Unfinished Life: An Autobiography. New York, NY: Harper & Bros.

Index